# The Blitzed City

# The Blitzed City

*The Destruction of Coventry, 1940*

By Karen Farrington

Aurum
Press

First published in Great Britain 2015 by Aurum Press Ltd
74—77 White Lion Street
Islington
London N1 9PF

www.aurumpress.co.uk

A catalogue record for this book is available from the British Library.

ISBN 978 1 78131 325 1

eBook ISBN 978 1 78131 480 7

2015 2017 2019 2018 2016

1 3 5 7 9 10 8 6 4 2

Typeset in ITC New Baskerville by Saxon Graphics Ltd, Derby

Printed and bound by CPI Group (UK) Ltd, Croydon, CR0 4YY

# Author's Note

Few stories stir the heart like those of survival in the face of adversity. Seventy-five years ago, Coventry and its people endured a punishing air attack that left hundreds of people dead. Thousands more thought they were going to die that night as a blizzard of bombs fell indiscriminately, hitting homes and industry. This is a story of ordinary people in extraordinary times and it is told by the people who were there. These are the illuminating accounts of Dennis Adler, Eileen Bees, Janice Chapman, Len and Cecilia Dacombe, Betty Daniel, Marjorie Edge, Alan Hartley, Mary Heath, Mary Latham, Eric Lloyd, John Sargent and Christina and Len Stephenson. I am indebted to them for allowing me to raid their memory banks so extensively. Other accounts have been taken from numerous archives to give as broad a picture as possible of this shocking night and its grim consequences. Those that provided particular assistance were at the Imperial War Museums, the Herbert Gallery and the National Archives.

# Prologue

For stretcher-bearer Dennis Adler, it was a sight that would remain etched in his memory forever. Aged fifteen, he was already an old hand at working through the night as a volunteer cadet for the St John Ambulance Brigade. He had become accustomed to seeing crushed limbs and bloodied faces, and he could even carry a corpse without flinching. But the waiting room in front of him was like nothing he had witnessed before.

At first glance, it looked like a scene from a military hospital. As bombs plunged through buildings and flames reached the height of rooftops outside, the casualties who poured through the doors looked something like battlefield cannon fodder. Yet, this was not the aftermath of a campaign, nor was it combatants who were suffering such grievous injuries. It was the night of the Coventry Blitz and these victims were civilians who had become the collateral damage of a new phase of a terrifying, modern military struggle.

By day, Dennis Adler was employed helping a milkman to deliver dairy items by lorry to the nearby town of Kenilworth for the Co-op. He had already notched up jobs as an office boy and a factory hand, but it was outdoor employment that he relished and he had more in his weekly pay packet than the ten shillings a week he had previously earned.

He spent his afternoons asleep, and at night, he devoted hours to the Gulson Road Hospital in Coventry. It was a small municipal hospital with a single operating theatre the size of an average sitting room. Even in those times of crisis, there were no more than four doctors on duty.

Initially, he nearly missed this shift at the hospital. Fearful of the raid's early intensity, his father Harry had almost stopped him from going. As the family made its way to a shelter, Dennis had finally persuaded his father that it was appropriate for him to peel off and report for duty. Dennis did not realise, as he spoke kindly to one patient here and gave a drink to another there, that he had already delivered his last pint of milk. It would be weeks before Dennis left the hospital again.

More casualties arrived who needed his attention. This time, it was a mother with a baby in her arms. Both looked like they were sleeping serenely, but to his horror, Dennis suddenly realised that they were dead. A doctor explained that the invisible force of a bomb blast had killed them. They had died from internal injuries, although both were quite unmarked.

It was not only ambulances that brought patients to the hospital. Every kind of vehicle was used to ferry them in and more hobbled there on foot. Soon, there was no electricity to light the hospital, or water to mop up wounds. It became harder to administer even basic treatment to the streams of people in need.

Later, Dennis recognised some of the firemen being brought in with injuries. They had been stationed opposite his school and used to wave at pupils such as him. All of them died as the hospital struggled to cope, with people perishing from shock, for want of warmth, or for loss of blood.

Alarm at the mounting death toll made him pause for a moment. Then Dennis pulled himself together and helped to move bodies away from the main waiting area to make room for more patients. That night he – along with numerous others – worked tirelessly for the very survival of the city and its people.

# Introduction

On a frosty Thursday night in the winter of 1940, Coventry was laid waste by an aerial bombardment. Today, terror among civilians sparked by a thunderous rain of bombs from high-flying aircraft is a harsh reality that happens on an alarmingly regular basis. Back then, the grim art of the Blitz was in its infancy. Until that fateful raid aeroplanes tended to travel in twos or tens rather than in hundreds. Bombs were getting bigger, but they were still comparatively modest in size. The chances of hitting a target with one that had been launched from an aeroplane at high altitude were slim, as accurate navigation was too often a matter of luck for a pilot and his crew. Conversely, any defence against enemy fliers was still largely ineffectual.

The devastation of Coventry – acclaimed worldwide as a medieval gem – marked the moment that the bomber came of age. Before that moment on 14 November, both sides clung precariously to the moral high ground, claiming their targets were military ones. When the truth of the matter was consistently proved – that bombs fell indiscriminately on the civilian population as well as the munitions factories they worked in – an idea formed in the minds of those planning the attacks: why not bomb the people who were making armaments as well as the armaments themselves, to crush their spirits, create pandemonium and thus bring a speedy end to the conflict?

Although it was not the first city to be bombarded – and it certainly would not be the last – the attack on Coventry changed

1

the tenor of aerial warfare. London had been Blitzed, but the city was too sprawling for the terror to be a game changer. Coventry was smaller and more compact. If the terrible effects of a concentrated attack could be maximised anywhere, it was there and German air chiefs were keen to experiment with this new tactic.

The Luftwaffe not only used incendiaries to best effect but also its navigational technology, which, although far from foolproof, was way ahead of that of the British. It had the means to get pilots to the correct location and help them aim their bombs. Consequently, the facts and figures of the ferocious dusk-to-dawn raid are brutal.

Between 30,000 and 40,000 incendiaries fell on both military and civilian targets. Most were standard blaze-setters, but about a fifth had a delaying device that then caused an explosion in the face of fire fighters, inflicting burns and blindness. More than 503 tons of high explosives tumbled through the night sky, in an estimated 16,000 bombs – some of which weighed as much as 1,102lb. In addition, fifty parachute mines, each weighing in at 2,205lb and containing 1,543lb of high explosives, were dropped.

It is thought that 568 people were killed out of a population of 238,000, with a further 863 seriously injured. The circumstances of their demise are shocking, with people burned, crushed, shocked or frightened to death. The true figures may never be known and the city is still dogged by rumours that the death toll was much higher.

Yet the story of the attack on the city is not just about a switch of strategies by German High Command and those who perished in terror that night because of it. It is the tales of those who survived, drawing on inner resourcefulness and iron will, that make the event so memorable. Not everyone was a hero, although there were many who emerged as such from the fire and the chaos. Nor was there a higher-than-average proportion of cowardice. Most people fell between the two extremes, ordinary people coping as best they could in appalling conditions. And what the city had in abundance was people.

Coventry was a busy city because it was the beating heart of industrial England. It was heavy with engineering works prior to the war and became more so as the conflict unfolded. Without Coventry and other cities like it, Britain would not have had the means to fight a war. And cities like Coventry needed men – and women – to make them tick.

It was not everyone's first choice to stay on a factory production line. There was evidently some sense of adventure in signing up for the services at the outbreak of war, swapping shabby civvies for a smart uniform, despite the obvious perils. No doubt men heading over to France in 1939 thought the home-based factory hands had a cushy number. However, it was claimed that for every fighting soldier or airman no fewer than seven munitions workers were needed to keep him properly supplied.

A year later, when the remnants of the British Expeditionary Force had returned to home soil and there was not a land-based battle in sight, it was those in engineering who were subjected to enemy attack along with their wives and children, rather than uniformed soldiers.

Now these men whose job on the home front – considered mundane in peace time – made them essential workers could not have signed up as soldiers even if they tried. The industrial muscle that kept the country afloat was inevitably unglamorous and largely went uncelebrated. Those who stayed home to keep production buoyant were financially well rewarded. At a time when coal miners in South Wales were paid only £3 per week, Coventry aircraft workers were bringing home much more than the national average wage of £4 per week, although they were working a sixty-five-hour week to do so.

Ultimately, no amount of income could protect cities and those within them from the attentions of enemy aircraft during the Second World War. There had been aerial attacks in the First

World War, which caused unprecedented alarm, but they did not compare to the scale or intensity of what occurred in the war that erupted little more than twenty years afterwards.

As more men were needed in the services, so the women across Britain stepped up to take their places in the factories and, by 1941, women had been conscripted into aircraft factories, with the reluctant agreement of the unions.

As the heart of England became its front line for a night, the perspective of the people of Coventry was irrevocably changed as was the city itself. Housewives there developed an affinity for their counterparts in Warsaw and Rotterdam; factory workers knew what troops on the battlefield were experiencing and children understood what it was to live in a devastated war zone with all the shortages that that entailed. As a result of the timing of the raid, its intensity and the high rate of civilian casualties, the story of Coventry's Blitz became emblematic of them all.

It is why a forensic investigation into what happened that night and afterwards gives voice not only to Coventry but every other city that was bombed during the Second World War, and since.

## Chapter One

# 'The bomber will always get through'

*Stanley Baldwin*

For centuries manned flight was nothing but a distant dream pondered by intellectuals and scientists alongside the ambitious, the brave and the downright foolhardy. They watched birds soaring overhead and wondered how life would be enhanced if only mankind could mimic those aerial antics. Through the ages, men tried strapping on feathered wings, attaching themselves to kites, experimenting with rotor blades and even flirting with the idea of gliders. A few even threw themselves from towers to put flawed designs to the test.

Yet even the noblest of dreams can have unintended consequences, and if those aspiring aviators had known what lay ahead, they might have been more careful about what they wished for. When it finally arrived, the reality of manned flight proved to be both a blessing and a curse.

Initially, the prospect of easy, speedy travel across countries and continents seemed to bring universal benefit, but a few short years after man's ingenuity took him soaring above the clouds, the military saw ominous potential. From that point, it was a devastating new weapon that could rain death from the skies hundreds of miles from home territory.

Senior officers and eager engineers began toying with the notion of using aerial advantage to unlock a swift victory in military conflicts. Within a few short decades a new age had dawned, where strategic bombing became the norm. (Ultimately, the term 'strategic' – which implied a theoretical purpose or design beyond widespread destruction – could be substituted by area, tactical, precision, carpet or terror.)

The ensuing losses among pilots and aircrew – brave young men killed at a tender age – were shocking. But the death toll among the professionals has been dwarfed by the number of people on all sides who have died in the past century beneath a Blitz of bombs, either in their homes, or at their workplaces or while taking shelter from the onslaught.

However, if the generals and politicians of the early twentieth century believed aviation technology would make war redundant, they were wrong. Air superiority has never been sufficient to finish a war once it has begun, although there were plenty who convinced themselves otherwise.

Before the Second World War, the British Prime Minister Stanley Baldwin was in the vanguard of these people, when he issued a dire warning:

> I think it is well also for the man in the street to realise that there is no power on earth that can protect him from being bombed. Whatever people may tell him, the bomber will always get through. The only defence is in offence, which means that you have to kill more women and children more quickly than the enemy if you want to save yourselves...
>
> But when the next war comes, and European civilisation is wiped out, as it will be, and by no force more than that force, then do not let them lay blame

on the old men. Let [young pilots] remember that
they, principally, or they alone, are responsible for the
terrors that have fallen upon the earth.

During the 1930s, when Baldwin was making his point, the
thought of a war dominated by aerial bombers was feared
much as nuclear war would be in the 1950s and 1960s. It's
worth assessing the short history of flight that had unfolded
in Baldwin's lifetime to understand why he was fearful.

At the outset, manned flight as a tool of annihilation was
a long way from the minds of those engaged in the drive to
push back the barriers of science. Pioneers like these were
fuelled by what sometimes seemed to be an insurmountable
challenge. A desire among those in ancient civilisations to
take to the air was evident in the fabric of the fables they
produced, the most memorable of which was of Icarus
coming down to earth with a fatal bump after flying too close
to the sun with wings made from feathers and wax.

For years, it seemed that the only option was to mimic
birds. But as the centuries wore on, fresh ideas gradually
came to the table. Leonardo da Vinci, now renowned for
being ahead of his time, made more than 100 drawings that
illustrated his ambitions about flight, mostly centred on what
he termed an Ornithopter. Although it was never made in
his lifetime, it might be seen as a distant ancestor of the
modern helicopter.

Skip forward a few more centuries and the first major
development appeared, the hot air balloon, invented by
brothers Joseph and Jacques Etienne Montgolfier in 1783.

For the first time, men and women could take to the air to
enjoy the panoramic views and hitherto unknown speeds of
travel; beautiful, undoubtedly, and breathtakingly impressive.

And quickly the military made use of them, with a tethered balloon forming part of the defences during the French Revolutionary Wars and silk balloons featuring in the American Civil War.

During the 1870 Siege of Paris – when Baldwin was an infant – balloons were a symbol of resistance after rampant Prussian forces had beaten a path to the gates of the French capital city and isolated it from the rest of the country. Inevitably, there were soon woeful shortages of food and information. Yet the city had some talented technicians who could construct a new hot air balloon every twelve days when they worked at full stretch. Then, the aim was to pilot one of the craft to an unoccupied area to discharge important messages and intelligence. More than sixty balloons, with at least 110 passengers, went aloft during the five-month siege, doing valuable reconnaissance work in the process.

Consequently, the first anti-aircraft guns were developed by the Prussians in an effort to fell the balloons and gain an upper hand in this new and unfamiliar manner of warfare.

Steel baron Alfred Krupp modified a 1-pounder gun and installed it on the back of a horse-drawn carriage. Known as the *ballonkanone*, it proved to be the humble beginnings of an entirely new facet of military hardware.

Balloons then evolved into powered airships which could be dispatched in chosen directions rather than remain at the whim of the wind. The process of evolution continued when planes were developed in the first decade of the twentieth century after the Wright brothers' historic flight in 1903. Though not everyone could see the potential in military terms: Field Marshal Ferdinand Foch, who was considered to be one of the best military minds of his generation in France, believed flying to be a sport rather than a military strategy.

The neighbouring Italians begged to differ. A relatively new country with major ambitions, Italy initiated a war against the Ottoman Empire in North Africa with the unashamed intention of carving out an empire. In doing so, it became the first nation to flirt with aerial bombardment.

On 1 November 1911, two months after the start of the conflict, Lieutenant Giulio Gavotti flew from an airfield in what is now Libya over the Ain Zara oasis with four round grenade-style bombs in the cockpit of his Etrich Taube plane, each weighing about 3lb. Three were nestling in a lined, leather case on the floor while a fourth was snug in his flying jacket. As he approached his target, the trail-blazing aviator kept one hand on the wheel while using the other to lay the bomb from his jacket in his lap. Then he ripped out the safety catch and tossed it over the side of the German-made aircraft, carefully avoiding the wing. As dark clouds rose from the tents below, Gavotti threw out two more bombs before flying to a military camp near Tripoli and dispatching the fourth. No one was hurt in the raid, but Gavotti had set down a marker in what turned out to be a victorious campaign and was lauded for doing so. The following year, he undertook the world's first night-time mission.

The Italians also deployed airships in a war that is mainly significant for revealing the weaknesses of the failing Ottoman Empire. At the time, airships had been flying for longer than aeroplanes and had at least as much military consequence. Their reputation and potential were largely down to innovative thinking by German innovators. By the turn of the twentieth century, Count Ferdinand von Zeppelin was working on what was effectively a motorised balloon. It was his idea to develop the bullet-shaped airship, and his

LZ1 made its maiden flight on 2 July 1900. It travelled three and a half miles in eighteen minutes, thanks to two 14 horsepower (hp) engines, with two gondoliers slung beneath to house the crew.

Abundant modifications in construction were made to ensuing models, and the future of the Zeppelin seemed assured until the doomed LZ4 was destroyed in 1908 on home turf by a storm as it attempted a twenty-four-hour endurance flight. This might have signalled the end for the airship, but the German public, imbued with patriotic fervour for the venture, donated six million marks to build the next one. So successful was the Zeppelin that all airships became known by this name, even when some were made by another manufacturer.

Initially, the aim was to provide passenger transport, but with the onset of the First World War, the potential for military engagement became quickly apparent. Airships were almost immediately deployed by Germany in the Low Countries and five months later the first air raids were unleashed on British soil. An initial foray was made on 19 January 1915 when two airships set off from Germany with 30 hours' worth of fuel, eight bombs and twenty-five incendiary devices. Kaiser Wilhelm II would not give his permission for it to bomb London, where his cousin King George V lived. But his sensitivities were not sufficient to stop the bombing of Great Yarmouth and Kings Lynn, two targets on the east coast of England that so far had been touched by the war only through the departure of their young men to the Western Front.

After lighting a path with the incendiaries, the crews bombed these comparatively rural outposts and killed nine people. Furthermore, they created panic among residents who had expected a seaborne invasion rather than one from the skies. It was, of course, a completely unknown concept to those on the ground, although there had been attacks on east-coast towns from ships so far out at sea that they could not be seen, which had evoked similar levels of shock. Still, people everywhere, subjected to rumours about sightings of the gas giants, were filled with dread at the thought of aerial bombardment, a condition flippantly known as 'Zeppelinitis'.

More raids followed, and eventually the Germans extended their range by the end of May to include London and other cities. Zeppelins swooped in virtual silence, having killed the throb of their engines at an appropriate moment. Looming above the chimneys, they disposed of their payload, then rose swiftly into the clouds after firing up once more. The effect of these sinister sights on the ground caused dread and curiosity. Londoners fled to shelter in the Underground stations, behaviour that was initially frowned upon by the authorities who were concerned that it would hinder the transport system. Eventually, the government relented, although posters made it clear that birds, dogs, cats and, oddly, mail carts were not permitted in stations. One estimate put the number of Londoners seeking overnight shelter from the Zeppelin raids at 300,000.

At first, there were no defences that could counter the threat. Guns on the ground did not have the range or the agility to shoot down a high and moving target. But, as always, warfare brought forth new defensive as well as attacking technologies. Artillery became more powerful, not least to counter the threat that airships posed to the trenches, and searchlights were installed in cities to illuminate targets. A blackout was declared in major cities. Barrage balloons, which resembled airships but were tethered to the ground, were also sent up around London. The balloons, sometimes armed with explosives, were on steel cables strong enough to bring down low-flying craft. Sometimes, a cable was also strung horizontally between balloons to trip up the incoming enemy.

As time went by, Zeppelins, which had once stolen in over the British coast unseen and untroubled, found themselves spotted by coastal observation stations and ships and their radio messages monitored by listening stations. It meant an alarm could be sounded after warnings were phoned through to the Admiralty in London and aeroplanes in the home defence force – generally speaking the BE2c bi-plane – could be scrambled. Now armed with incendiary bullets, lone pilots had plenty to aim at as they tried to ignite the gases that kept the Zeppelin in the sky.

Indeed, more aircraft than ever were devoted to countering the airship menace. In June 1915, a British fighter pilot brought down an airship for the first time by dropping bombs on its roof. Now, it was the turn of the machine guns that defended the airships to appear clunky, although it was some time before the feat of 1915 was repeated.

As far as civilians went, however, the threat remained a considerable one. One London woman wrote to her mother in Devon after witnessing a raid and told her how the city sky was illuminated by fire:

> It's a wonder that I'm alive today and I must confess that last night I thought it was all up with us. I don't want to alarm you, mother, but it's no good concealing facts, is it? One of the Zepps was almost over our house, and a terrible cannonading was going on all around. It is impossible to describe it all and you could never

imagine what it was like. I have never spent such an awful half hour before and I was horribly frightened. In fact, we all were, even the boys. I am jolly glad you were not there, dear.

The Zepps got right into the city this time and did heaps of damage around Liverpool Street and Wood Street. There must have been more than one because they seem to have been nearly all over London last night.

The excitement was terrible, people were rushing about in the street, half dressed. Whistles were blowing and specials were going around ordering all lights out. It started just before 11. None of us had gone to bed when suddenly we heard a terrific noise quickly followed by the loud booming of guns.

Instantly there was confusion and I knew at once it was Zepps. One of the boys ordered us all into the passage, turned out the lights and opened the doors for we could tell that the Zepp was jolly near. There we waited with white faces listening to the awful booming outside and expecting the house to topple down on us at any minute. I can't describe the sensation, it was simply awful.

Despite the threat, these observers were desperate to witness the scene:

We rushed into the garden and there, almost above us, was the Zepp. It was far different to what I expected to see and it was a great sight. Imagine a long, cigar-shaped car lighted up by the searchlights and surrounded by the starry blue sky. It was hard to realise that it was on such a desperate errand and we gazed, fascinated.

The shells from the anti aircraft guns were bursting all around and each boom sent an awful thrill through us. I shall never forget that night.

As for the airship crew, which numbered about twenty, they were dressed in thick winter clothing to guard against the freezing temperatures that they experienced as they flew high above the earth. At first, the hit-and-run missions seemed safe enough. But as Britain resolved her air defence issues, there were more casualties, and eventually the hearts of everyone aboard were thumping with fear while the raids were in progress. After a number of costly Zeppelins were brought down, these air raids began to peter out. More than fifty had taken place, involving 115 airships with losses among crew running at about 40 per cent. About a quarter of the raids were over London, with some raids taking place in the Midlands, including one in Coventry, and a few in Scotland.

But it wasn't the only method of attack from the air suffered in Britain. German aircraft raided the nation's shores as early as 1914 and these became larger and more robust as the conflict wore on, especially so when the hopes invested in airships began to vanish. Their visits caused still more casualties. Raids like the one on 25 May 1917, when twenty-three Gotha bombers dispensed bombs over southeast England during the night (increasingly the favoured time for sorties), served to lower morale among the British population. With the final death toll from both types of air aid topping 1,400 it is easy to see why the government feared the raids would undermine the war effort.

Of course, Britain was in possession of aeroplanes at the outbreak of the war and they did not stand idly by. In 1914, before the appearance of airships over British shores, there were a series of raids on Zeppelin sheds to destroy the new-age weapons. However, German Zeppelins went on to bomb targets in Greece and Bucharest in 1916. There were abundant cries of 'foul play' from those on the ground because at the time there were protocols in place governing the conduct of war. In the last half of the nineteenth century, there had been growing disquiet among the thinking classes about the fate of soldiers on the battlefield, both in Europe and during the American Civil War. As the age of set-piece skirmishes diminished, there seemed a growing need to codify behaviour in war towards soldiers and civilians. The results were a series of Geneva Conventions and Hague Conventions, which ran parallel to curb military excesses.

The first legislation to limit aerial attacks was drawn up as early as 1899 and is known as the Hague Convention II. One of its declarations specifically states that those powers signing up are forbidden, for five years, from launching 'projectiles and explosives from balloons or by other new methods of similar nature'. The Convention was renewed in 1907. Moreover, land and air warfare were bracketed together as far as the bombardment of undefended towns was concerned. Surprise attacks were also prohibited. The commander of an attacking force was obliged to warn the authorities of an intended target about what was to take place. But the development of aeroplanes soon outran even these plans for possible legislation, let alone any signed and sealed international agreement, as each new model had ever greater capabilities.

Then in 1911, the Madrid Resolution declared that aerial warfare was legal provided that it met certain conditions and was not more destructive than war on land or at sea. With the rapid advances in aircraft technology, there was an unwillingness among countries to sign up to something that might ultimately hamper their ambitions. Some experts were certain that air supremacy would guarantee victory. Lieutenant Colonel Giulio Douhet, a notable military theorist, expounded his beliefs in a 1921 book called *The Command of the Air.* Surprisingly, he was an army man rather than an early pilot, but he was convinced of the virtue of military aircraft. Defence against air raids from anti-aircraft guns and fighters was pointless, he declared, and all efforts should be devoted to corralling more powerful aerial bombing forces than any neighbouring country. A second edition of the book, published in 1927, was translated into English, French, German and Russian and became a standard military text. He was perhaps correct in assuming that aeroplanes were offensive weapons par excellence. Accurately, he predicted that 'the battlefield will be limited only by the boundaries of the nations at war, and all of their citizens will become combatants, since all of them will be exposed to the aerial offensives of the enemy'. But his pessimistic scenarios for aerial warfare were fortunately flawed. He wrongly believed that a combination of fires and poison gases dispensed by attacking aircraft would leave entire regions paralysed: 'A complete breakdown of the social structure cannot but take place in a country subjected to this kind of merciless pounding from the air. The time will soon come when, to put an end to the horror and suffering, the people themselves, driven by the instinct of self-preservation, would rise up and demand an end to the war – this before their Army and Navy had time to mobilize.'

The political classes did take note, however, and some sought to counter the threat. The result was the Hague Rules of Air Warfare, produced in 1923 – but never ratified by countries still reluctant to rein in the new and exciting aerial weapon now tantalisingly within their grasp. Had it been signed and sealed, this new set of rules would have restricted aerial bombardment to military targets and outlawed attacks on cities and towns. In cases where military targets were embedded in civilian populations, the code categorically declared 'the aircraft must abstain from bombardment'.

In another article of the proposed rules, there was an avowed aim to protect historic sites: 'In bombardment by aircraft all necessary steps must be taken by the commander to spare as far as possible buildings dedicated to public worship, art, science, or charitable purposes, historic monuments, hospital ships, hospitals, and other places where the sick and wounded are collected, provided such buildings, objects or places are not at the time used for military purposes.'

They were wonderful sentiments from well-meaning negotiators, but they amounted to nothing without the relevant signatures. Thus, as Europe shaped up for its second major conflict in just over two decades, there was nothing to dissuade the hawks among the air force commanders from unleashing the horrific weapons at their disposal.

As it was, the size of national air forces grew and their actions remained unfettered by legislation. Britain began radically expanding her air capability from 1934 and, by 1936, had reorganised in earnest to meet a growing threat from Germany, creating bomber, fighter and coastal commands.

Following the First World War the Germans had been prohibited from having aircraft by the terms of the Treaty of Versailles, but under Hitler's leadership, they disregarded its provisions and the Luftwaffe was unveiled in 1935. Despite this development and the regional threat it represented, there is evidence that Hitler was at first reluctant to embrace the potential of aerial bombing in warfare. In 1935, he told one correspondent: 'War has been speeded up too much and made too overwhelmingly destructive for our geographical limitations. Within an hour – in some instances within forty minutes – of the outbreak of hostilities swift bombing machines would wreak ruin upon European capitals.'

Certainly, the newly wrought Luftwaffe operated differently from Britain's Royal Air Force, which had been formed in 1918. Rather than categorise its aircraft by function, the Germans operated Luftflotten in territories. According to Air Chief Marshall Sir Arthur Tedder, the Germans never learned to use their Luftwaffe to best effect. But it wasn't for want to trying. Moreover, the Germans were already flirting with the idea of bombing civilians rather than military targets.

The bombing of Guernica in Spain stands out as the starkest legacy of a diplomatic failure which resulted in the lack of international laws governing aerial assaults. Spain became embroiled in a civil war from 1936 as Nationalists led by General Francisco Franco tried to overthrow the Republican government. The conflict became a focus of the right–left fissure that was splitting Europe at the time. The Republicans attracted the support of the International Brigade, typically comprising idealists, writers, artists and others. Franco called on the support of Hitler, by now the undisputed ruler of Germany, who was re-arming his country at speed. To Spain, the Führer dispatched the Condor Legion, an off-shoot of the as yet untested Luftwaffe. On 26 April 1937, at the behest of Franco, German airmen, helped by counterparts from Fascist Italy, unleashed a rehearsal of the chaos that would soon blight much of Europe.

Guernica was close to Republican forces, but could not be categorised as a military base. Indeed, on the Monday the attack happened, it had been bustling with market-goers. Although the attack came in several waves, the primary damage was caused in just fifteen minutes in the late afternoon as three bomber squadrons attacked the town. At the same time, biplanes were strafing the roads leading out of the town, shooting anyone who tried to flee. For years, the death toll was said to be 1,650, although the figure has been revised downwards since the 1970s and currently the total is generally thought to be around 300. But the sense of shock was palpable. In Britain, a Gaumont newsreel told cinema goers: 'This was a city and these were homes, like yours.'

Afterwards, Franco's forces blamed Republicans for destroying the town with explosives as they retreated. It was the journalists present, most memorably George Steer from *The Times*, who helped to set the record straight. Steer became a champion of the Basque population – which suffered as a minority no matter who was in power – and wrote strikingly about this unacceptable new face of warfare. From shell-shocked victims and terrified refugees, Steer drew extraordinary testimony:

> In the form of its execution and the scale of the destruction it wrought ... the raid on Guernica is unparalleled in military history. Guernica was not a military objective. A factory producing war material lay outside the town and was untouched. So were two barracks some distance from the town. The town lay

far behind the lines. The object of the bombardment was seemingly the demoralization of the civil population and the destruction of the cradle of the Basque race.

On his trip to Guernica, Steer was accompanied by the *Daily Express* correspondent Noel Monks, who reported in similar terms. Monks' first task was to help Basque soldiers collect charred bodies that the flames had claimed:

> Some of the soldiers were sobbing like children. There were flames and smoke and grit, and the smell of burning human flesh was nauseating. Houses were collapsing into the inferno.
>
> In the Plaza, surrounded almost by a wall of fire, were about a hundred refugees. They were wailing and weeping and rocking to and fro. One middle-aged man spoke English. He told me: 'At four, before the market closed, many aeroplanes came. They dropped bombs. Some came low and shot bullets into the streets.'

Despite the power of the words dispatched by the British journalists, their versions were rebutted by Franco's aides who released false information through a powerful international network.

Guernica wasn't the first attack of its kind in Spain; Steer had witnessed the Condor Legion in action over Durango earlier the same year, leaving 158 dead. Barcelona was also repeatedly attacked by the Italian Air Force, but its citizens fared better with a network of underground tunnels providing shelters. It was not even the first episode of 'carpet' bombing on a civilian population. Western colonialist powers had used the technique in Africa and Steer himself had watched the Italian Air Force bomb the Ethiopians. (Poisonous gas dispensed from planes was the Italians' weapon of choice during this conflict.) But the famous painting produced by Pablo Picasso depicting the agony of its population has kept Guernica at the forefront of public consciousness.

Events in Spain and the appalling transgressions of the Italians in Africa served to underline the weaknesses of the League of Nations, the organisation established after the First World War to keep international peace. Further, there was the aerial bombing of Chinese cities, notably Shanghai in 1932 and 1937, by the Japanese during their stealthy invasion. From that city's international sector, British and American residents witnessed the wholesale killings of the Chinese population at close quarters. Hundreds perished, either from shrapnel injuries or after being trapped by falling buildings. Protestors in London, outraged by the deaths, were told by a speaker: 'The air raids in Canton and in Spain are only dress rehearsals for the air raids we may expect on London'.

The failure of diplomats charged with keeping world peace in dealing with the new and awesome aerial threat was by now painfully obvious to all. Flailing in the face of its inadequacies, the League of Nations nonetheless passed a unanimous resolution on 30 September 1938 concerning the protection of civilians from aerial warfare, calling for new and strict regulations. It reminded members that the intentional bombing of civilian populations was illegal, that targets must be both properly identifiable and legitimate military objectives and that any attack on such targets must be carried out in a way that ensured civilian populations in the neighbourhood were not bombed through negligence.

There was, however, a sense that the League of Nations' rules would amount to nothing if war broke out. To underline the point, the prominent peace campaigner Philip John Noel-Baker told Parliament on 21 June 1938, 'The only way to prevent atrocities from the air is to abolish air warfare and national air forces altogether.'

Although he eventually received the Nobel Peace Prize in 1959, the aspirations of this Labour politician and former Olympic athlete, who worked tirelessly for the League of Nations and its successor, the United Nations, seemed hopelessly wide of the mark. At the same time, the Assistant Chief of Air Staff was telling people that Britain should expect night raids by between 300 and 500 aircraft in any forthcoming conflict. Britain's Ministry of Health estimated hospital bed requirements following an air raid as between 1 million and 2.8 million. So the idea of Parliament adopting Noel-Baker's favoured option, disarmament, at this stage seemed a non-starter. Yet his views were shared by many, including a considerable number of city councillors in Coventry, who were members of the Labour Party and the Peace Movement. And his fears about the effects of aerial bombing were commonly held as tensions in the world rose.

With the anticipation of war rife, there was a grave tendency to fear the worst. In June 1939, the Air Raid Defence League issued a pamphlet that claimed the number of casualties in a single day's raiding was likely to be 35,000, a figure that would increase to 100,000 in a few days.

A year earlier, Professor J. B. S. Haldane wrote a book called *Air Raid Precautions* with the intention of giving his informed comments to ordinary people. Haldane, a scientist, had been injured by a bomb during the First World War and travelled three times to Spain during the Civil War to investigate how the population protected itself in air raids. His upper estimate for casualties during a major raid was 100,000 and he gave a no-holds-barred view of its dreadful aftermath: 'Air raids are not only wrong. They are loathsome and disgusting. If you had ever seen a child smashed by a bomb into something like a mixture of dirty rags and cat's meat you would realise this fact as intensely as I do.'

But higher-profile personalities than Haldane also warned of the threat posed by unrestrained aerial warfare. The American President Franklin D. Roosevelt encompassed the thoughts of most concerned people at the start of the Second World War, having witnessed the destruction of Guernica.

The ruthless bombing from the air of civilians in unfortified centers of population ... has sickened the hearts of every civilized man and woman, and has profoundly shocked the conscience of humanity .... I am therefore addressing this urgent appeal to every Government which may be engaged in hostilities publicly to affirm its determination that its armed forces shall in no event, and under no circumstances, undertake the bombardment from the air of civilian populations.

For a surprisingly long time, his plea for proper thought among the protagonists held sway. But ultimately, even he could not prevent the inevitable slide into macho military muscle-flexing inspired by air power.

# Chapter Two

# 'Sent to Coventry'

*English saying*

Although the Coventry area was thought to have been settled as early as the Bronze Age, it remained sparsely populated for many years. The Domesday Book, a record made sometime after the Saxon era, indicated the five hides of land labelled Coventry had a population of about seventy. Indeed, there were many more trees than people, the area being part of the Forest of Arden. The story of Lady Godiva, who allegedly rode naked through the streets to prevent her husband from imposing a tax on the people of Coventry, has been much embellished.

Perhaps the main significance of the Godiva of common folklore is that she was a woman who refused to admit defeat, like so many Coventry women a thousand years later during the Second World War.

Her character may have been based on a woman of significance with relatively loose connections to Coventry called Godgifu, who married one Earl Leofric, although there's little to connect her with horseback notoriety.

Leofric was one of King Cnut's right-hand men. Godgifu was wealthy in her own right before she married Leofric and became one of the richest landowners in the country after inheriting his wealth when he died in 1057, a right that seems to have been lost to women after the Norman Conquest in 1066.

It is known that the couple did invest in the church, paying for a Benedictine monastery in Coventry from 1043 and furnishing its coffers. But the story of the naked ride doesn't appear until long after her death, which came in 1067. And it was centuries later that the folk tale was embellished with the story of Peeping Tom – the tailor who defied her request not to peer out of the window as she passed and was blinded by heavenly wrath.

Godiva may or may not have existed, but her significance to Coventry is real enough. For years she has been a symbol of the city, lending her name to civic processions, swimming clubs and even city-made hosiery.

Coventry, like many other sites in England, started to expand from its humble origins and, by the twelfth century, it boasted a castle once taken by King Stephen during a dispute. Coventry's earls apparently held sway over half the neighbourhood, while the other half was under the control of the Church, although within a century, the distinct spheres of nobles and Church became united behind a single defensive wall.

In 1345, Coventry was awarded a charter of incorporation when its first merchant guilds were in operation, and later it won county and city status. Reflecting its eminence, Parliament met twice there in the middle of the fifteenth century.

After becoming a prominent feature on England's religious map, Coventry attracted Franciscan and Carmelite monks; one set favouring grey robes and the other white. In their wake came the medieval trades, especially textiles; weavers, dyers and merchants came to the town and there was a healthy stock of fulling mills spaced along the River Sherbourne, helping to support a population of some 6,500. But those boom times were relatively short-lived. With the collapse of the local wool trade coinciding with the dissolution of the monasteries by Henry VIII, Coventry lost its vibrancy. The pall in fortunes chimed with a darker side of the city's history, too, with seven Lollards – critics of the established church – burnt at the stake for heresy in 1519. Protestant martyrs died the same grisly way in Coventry in the 1550s and the doomed Mary, Queen of Scots, was imprisoned there in 1569.

The dawn of the new century offered little comfort. Coventry citizens fell victim to one of the last waves of the bubonic plague to sweep the country, with almost 500 people dying in 1603. Soon afterwards, Coventry played its part in the Gunpowder Plot of 1605. Radical Catholics were planning to overthrow the English King, James I in London for, although his mother and his wife were Catholic, he had been brought up a Protestant and suppressed the Papacy. The intention was to place his young daughter, Princess Elizabeth, on the throne instead of him after she had been forcibly married to a powerful Catholic of their choosing. However, the princess was spirited away from her Warwickshire home to the walled safety of Coventry on the night that the plot began unravelling. Much later, Elizabeth – who was the sister of the ill-fated King Charles I – married a German prince.

During the English Civil War, Coventry was in the Parliamentarian camp. A host of Royalist prisoners taken at Cannock Chase were dispatched to the city, where they were given the cold shoulder by local people, giving rise to the saying 'sent to Coventry'. Perhaps, by way of retribution for this perceived lack of loyalty, King Charles II, whose father

King Charles I was executed by the Parliamentarians, ordered that Coventry's city walls be smashed down. By 1793, a barracks had been built on Smithford Street which became home to the Dragoon Guards and, later, the Royal Artillery.

But it was not for its military pedigree that Coventry became renowned. In the eighteenth century, industry once again came to the fore, with ribbon- and watch-making assuming dominant positions in the city's economy. Communications improved with the expansion of the canal system that embraced Coventry and the new stage-coach service that linked it with London. By 1801, its population had reached 16,000.

In the 1850s, the watch-making trade employed some 2,000 people, with one company alone turning out 9,000 watches a year. Eventually, American- and Swiss-made watches began cornering the market, and Coventry's watchmakers were forced to adapt, turning their skills to producing sewing machines – although the demand for machines also appeared to have a limited shelf life. So once again, Coventry's industries peaked and declined – but now there were more and newer technologies to fill the breach.

As the sewing-machine makers moved on, so the bicycle manufacturers moved in and Coventry became the home of Singer's 'Challenge' series of penny farthings, deemed an improvement on the French boneshakers that were imported at the time.

In 1885, the invention of the cycle chain led to a new breed of bicycles, made by various manufacturers, commonly called 'Safety' cycles to mark them out from their more hazardous predecessors. Cycling was the sport embraced by the burgeoning middle classes and its popularity soared. Soon the range available included the Apollo, the tricycle and an Imperial Club tandem, each lovingly forged in small factories in the city centre where metal was heated in compact furnaces and hammered into shape.

An advertisement for a Club tandem, which appeared in 1885, claimed that one company, Coventry Machinists, were makers of cycles for the Prince of Wales, the Empress of Russia, the Empress of Austria, the Sultan of Morocco and the King of Siam. Thus at the close of the nineteenth century, Coventry was the cycling capital of the world, with some fifty manufacturers.

But cycling, too, had soon had its day. Emerging from the wings this time was the motoring industry, providing the city with a major economic boom of national significance. Indeed, the first car made in Britain was manufactured at Daimler in Coventry in 1897, establishing a new and durable economic era that lasted for some seventy years.

George Singer's company, which had formed in 1874 to produce sewing machines and then bicycles, remained a part of it. It finally evolved into a motor manufacturer, becoming one of 142 car companies registered down the years in the city.

As early as 1911 there were 7,000 workers in Coventry's motor industry and it was the region's largest employer. These engineering skills, garnered in peacetime for economic expansion, became crucial with the onset of war. During the First World War, munitions factories were established in the city, which employed local men and women and workers from Ireland. They made 15-inch naval guns, gun mountings, fuse heads for artillery ammunition and howitzers. Some 500 planes were built in Coventry's new aircraft factories, which were established in 1917 and a further 2,000 engines were built or overhauled there.

It was perhaps for this reason that Coventry was subject to a single Zeppelin raid, on 12 April 1918, when an L62 drifted over the city, but it seems little damage was done.

Men who worked in these factories wore a brown armband embellished with a red crown, denoting that they were essential workers rather than army shirkers. It meant that they were not publicly presented with a white feather, the symbol of cowardice, which was freely given out on the street by those who themselves never saw front-line action. For the first time, considerable numbers of women also flocked to work in factories to aid the war effort, when previously they had worked primarily in service as kitchen or household helpers.

Yet it would be a mistake to suggest that Coventry's contribution to the war effort lay purely on the factory floor. By the end of the conflict, approximately 3,500 sons of the city had died in the trenches and, in 1921, the War Memorial Park was opened to honour them.

While the rest of the country suffered economic hardship at the end of the First World War, Coventry's manufacturing prowess held it in good stead. It developed a reputation for prosperity and job opportunities and, between the wars, people moved there from across Britain to find work. Many families were affected by the 1926 General Strike, which was compounded by economic depression three years later.

Numerous workers came from Barrow-in-Furness, for example, where the ship building industry had gone into decline, and from Lancashire, where the cotton mills were falling idle arrived in Coventry. Miners from the Scotland, the north and South Wales also headed for the city.

In the early Thirties, one penniless family man – who had not worked since the miners' strike in 1926 – walked from his home near the Welsh pits to the Midlands. On his arrival in Birmingham, he asked at a police station as to where he might find a bed for the night and the kindly policemen offered him a cell and a warm breakfast. The next day, when they discovered he was a miner, they directed him to a colliery in Coventry. Moreover, they had a whip-round to give him cash for a bus fare to get there. At Keresley Colliery, he got a job immediately and was soon joined by his family.

Perversely, it was this transient nature of Coventry's population that made Churchill, among others in war-time government, suspect the city – wrongly – of lacking 'civic pride'.

The Thirties were even more prosperous for Coventry than the Twenties. After 1931, when unemployment peaked at a fifth of the workforce, jobs became even more plentiful. Coventry's population then stood at 167,083, a rise of almost 40,000 people in a decade.

Housing was needed for the workers who made the industries tick – and fortunately there was plenty of it. Suburban areas were built from the middle of the nineteenth century onwards and, for the next 100 years, abundant and spacious housing was constructed until estates all but encircled the city. The first council houses were built in 1908 in a programme that was accelerated for munitions workers employed at the Ordnance factory in Red Lane and a mixture of private and public development gathered pace with the provision of new sewerage schemes. At the start of the Second World War, a new semi-detached home cost '£45 down and 13s 9d a week', which was well within the financial capabilities of a skilled factory worker. As the 1930s drew to a close, Coventry and its associated suburbs measured about five miles across and a similar distance north to south, with a population touching 238,000. At its heart was a mix of industry and housing existing cheek by jowl; not the product of any town planning, but an accidental evolution that occurred as history unfolded.

From 1936, industry was further expanded by 'shadow factories' on the city's outskirts, which were created to build army equipment. These were financed at least in part by the government (and run by existing companies) as a response to the expanding armoury in Nazi Germany. Shadow factories were established all over the country but, with nine built in Coventry, the city got more than its fair share. The Coventry-based industrialist William Rootes – who would later pilot the city's reconstruction – was chairman of the Shadow Industry Plan.

So, while it might not have been immediately clear to everyone at the time, the weight of industry in Coventry was dramatically increasing as Britain dragged itself back on to a war footing. It meant that people like Harry Adler, father of fifteen-year-old Dennis at Gulson Road Hospital on the night of the Blitz who, notorious for his trade union activities, could finally get a job after years of being blackballed by employers.

At the outbreak of the Second World War, about 38,000 people in Coventry were employed by the motor industry, many of them manning assembly lines. At the time, it cost about £150 to buy a small family car, putting it within the grasp of an increasing number of people, although there were still many more bicycles than cars on the roads. However, with its solid engineering pedigree, it was not just cars that were made in Coventry during the war years.

Hawker Siddeley, Vickers Armstrong, Armstrong Whitworth and Rolls-Royce were all producing aeroplanes or their engines and associated parts. The Merlin engine that would power the Spitfires and Hurricanes credited with winning the

31

battle of the skies were made in Coventry. At British Thomson-Houston, better known as BTH, in Ford Street, other aircraft parts were manufactured while Daimler, which had multiple sites, produced scout cars that played a leading role in the desert war of North Africa. Dunlop made wheels and tyres for aircraft as well as barrage balloons to hinder enemy aerial raids and anti-gas clothing. Later, underwater equipment for frogmen saboteurs was also made there.

At the General Electric Company (GEC), which also had a number of locations in the city, traditional munitions were made alongside VHF radio sets for fighter defence aircraft.

Parachutes were manufactured from the nylon produced by Courtaulds, while Coventry Climax made Civil Defence trailer pumps alongside emergency landing field generators for the RAF.

Fred Lee & Company – a former watchmaker – made industrial jewels that were essential to many processes and typical in compass bearings. Then there was Coventry Gauge and Tools Ltd, which eventually provided three-quarters of all the gauges used in the nation's armaments as well as a number of specialised tools. And behind this hefty front row of factories, there was a host of other small workshops and engineering outlets supplying the needs of these industrial giants.

So, unlike some other cities and towns, Coventry was full of young men of military-service age. This was accepted without question in the city, while in other areas men or their families were sometimes still presented with white feathers, in a legacy from the First World War.

Coventry was at least partly prepared for war.

Before the conflict broke out, many factories had anti-gas detectors in their yards, which were specially painted so that they would change colour if they were sprayed by the kinds of liquid gases used in the First World War. Comprehensive training lectures and drills were also undertaken, with many employers beefing up their auxiliary fire brigades and increasing the number of first-aid-trained staff on the premises. Prior to the National Fire Service, created in 1941, works brigades proliferated. They could be distinguished because, with the exception of the crew at Daimlers, they did not have a fire engine and used cars or trucks to tow water tenders to the scene of a blaze. For example, the Rootes fire team used an 18 hp Humber Hawk DDU 303 to haul the tender from place to place. In preparation for an aerial onslaught, buckets of sand and stirrup pumps were distributed everywhere. But, despite the apparent threat, few people left the city, not least because they were so well rewarded at work.

In the spring of 1939, Coventry's citizens, like those in other target areas, were offered Anderson shelters, which were free to manual workers covered by the National Insurance Acts or others earning less than £250 a year. Anderson shelters were intended for the garden and needed a 3-foot hole as well as some facilities for drainage. They were made of fourteen panels of curved and straight galvanised corrugated steel, standing 6ft high, 4ft 6in wide and 6ft 6in long. The panels were covered with soil to improve the level of protection they offered, and which consequently provided another place to grow flowers and vegetables.

Apart from hastily built public shelters, there were not many other alternatives. Indoor Morrison shelters were not distributed until 1941 – although, in Coventry, some historic buildings had cellars and others had underground storerooms. The installation of shelters formed a small part in the changing face of Coventry. On the outbreak of war, camouflage was draped over factories to help disguise them.

However, the vast growth in industry – hastened by the re-armament programme and endowing Coventry with about 300 factories – and the expansion of its housing estates had not been matched by a renewal in infrastructure. Coventry's medieval road system was unable to cope with the increasing volumes of traffic. There were some timber-framed houses and shops dating from the same period still huddled in the heart of the city, with a major slum clearance scheme to improve the centre deemed too expensive for the public purse. That said, some changes had been made as the city prospered in the twentieth century. A new Council House – as the civic centre was called – had been constructed as the First World War raged. And later the broad, new-look Corporation Street was built. It opened in 1931, after some city centre hovels had been pulled down. Then two roads – Great Butcher Row and Little Butcher Row – with their central gutters and overhanging first stories were demolished as part of the Trinity Street renovation.

In 1938, the industrialist Sir Alfred Herbert earmarked £100,000 to build a new gallery and museum, although plans were interrupted by the onset of war. However, large parts of a blueprint held by the city's architect's department before the war were little more than a wish-list for planners who dreamed of a city fit for the modern age.

Pressure on the traffic was partly eased by the opening in 1940 of the six-mile bypass south of Coventry between Ryton and Allesley, which kept traffic out of the city centre.

While there were plenty of improvements in the minds of planners, one thing they would not change was the three spires that defined the city, belonging to Christ Church, Holy Trinity and St Michael's, the latter having been elevated to the status of a cathedral in 1918. During the Second World

War, the Provost was R. T. Howard, who described the cathedral's grandeur as follows:

> It was one of the largest and most beautiful of all those churches built in England 600 years ago in the new style in which English builders had broken away from the lavish continental style to something peculiarly English in form.
>
> It was very spacious, [had] exquisite proportions of slender pillars, broad arches and large windows. It had the equal third tallest of all the spires in the country, perfectly decorated from the ground to the weathercock 300 ft above.

Coventry's high profile in Britain brought it some unwelcome attention as well, even before the arrival of Hitler's airmen. As newspapers and the airwaves were filled with dramatic accounts of how Hitler's troops had rolled into Poland and an invasion appeared to be imminent, there were other stories at the forefront of the minds of those living and working in Coventry.

The police had been on high alert for days, but they were not just on the lookout for rogue Nazis. Indeed, uniformed regulars and special constables, with their distinctive capes, had assiduously checked telephone kiosks, post boxes and railway arches for months after the Irish Republican Army declared war against Great Britain in January 1939, embarking on a campaign that its supporters dubbed the S plan. Duty constables sometimes accompanied postmen on their rounds, carrying a bucket of water to douse suspect packages.

Sadly, no one, uniformed or otherwise, had spotted a 5-lb boxed bomb, wrapped in brown paper and tied up with string, lying in a bicycle basket on 25 August. The Karriwell bicycle, costing £5 19s 6d, had been brought from Halford's in Smithson Street, loaded with its deadly cargo at a Coventry address and wheeled to Broadgate in the city centre where it was left, perched inconspicuously on a kerbside at the tail end of a busy Friday lunchtime. An alarm clock used as the timer was set to detonate the bomb shortly before 2.00 pm.

Five people died in the explosion. Twenty-one-year-old shop assistant Elsie Ansell was looking at jewellery in the window of H. Samuel's during a late lunch break when it occurred. She would not have noticed the bomb-laden bicycle as she surveyed the window display, her thoughts surely focused on her wedding day in a fortnight's time. Gwilym Rowlands, aged fifty, also had his head bowed, as he was sweeping the street. Known to everyone as Bill, he was at work as a Corporation cleaner outside Astley's and Burton with his colleague John Worth, who survived. The third and fourth victims were strolling back to work at W H Smith's after spending a lunch time together. Rex Gentle, aged thirty, and John Arnott, aged just fifteen, were killed alongside eighty-two-year-old James Clay, a printer still working despite his advanced years. More than fifty people were injured and the heart of the city was wrecked.

It was not the first IRA activity in Coventry. The city had been blasted in the spring along with numerous others in a spate of small-scale explosions designed to induce fear rather than fatalities. After announcing its intentions to terrorise, the IRA engineered more than 150 explosions around England that year.

When the English appeared largely unmoved by the campaign, the bombers became increasingly carefree about the possibility of civilian casualties. In July, a bomb was left at

Coventry's railway station as it thronged with people heading for summer excursions. Although many were shaken, no one was killed. The following day, another was detonated at Leicester's station. Despite these explosions in crowded venues, no one perished until the Broadgate bomb brought terror to Coventry's streets at the end of the summer.

There is good reason to believe it was a tragedy that nearly did not happen. Two weeks before the Broadgate attack, there had been a large explosion on some Coventry allotments. Two men ran from the scene and escaped by boarding a tram. They had accidentally detonated the stored explosives intended for the outrage.

Unfortunately, that did not put an end to the terrorists' plans, nor did it alert police to the impending disaster. It merely meant more explosive material had to be brought in from Liverpool at short notice. The bicycle was apparently deliberately parked in the city centre, although major IRA figures later insisted that the venue was a mistake.

The troubles that weighed down Coventry in those weeks must have made the city sag with a sorrow that was set apart from the impending war. However, a sense of unity and fortitude was taking shape alongside the horror that had taken innocent lives, never more so than when Elsie Ansell was buried at St Barbara's Church in Earlsdon, the church where she had intended to marry. She lay in her coffin in the fine white wedding dress in which she had planned to walk up the aisle. On top, lay a wreath of cream roses from her grief-stricken fiancé Harry Davies and surrounding it was an army of mourners some 700-strong.

The deaths in Coventry put paid to any lingering sympathies for a united Ireland in England. As a howl of fury arose, including public demonstrations on the city's streets, police set about finding the perpetrators. For many in the city centre that day, the sound of the IRA bomb going off was the first explosion they had ever heard. As the city's history continued to unfold in short order, it unfortunately would not be the last.

## Chapter Three

# 'The unbearable fetid smell of burned objects and the dust from crushed concrete made it difficult to breathe.'

### *A Warsaw Resident*

The Second World War began with Hitler's noisy and destructive invasion of Poland. Sirens attached to the wings of the Junkers Ju 87 attack aircraft wailed as they dive-bombed targets across the country announcing the outbreak of hostilities at dawn on 1 September. Hitler expressly ordered that the wind-driven sirens were used to cause confusion and panic in the population below. Known as Stukas, the planes provided a highly mobile airborne artillery that eradicated targets in the path of the fast-moving tanks in the Panzer divisions.

The Stuka – trialled by the Condor Legion in Spain – was sufficiently accurate to bomb roads and railway crossings because it flew so low. Although there was a danger that the pilot could black out from the brutal physical forces of acceleration as the plane plummeted through nine-tenths of its comparatively lofty cruising height, there were special dive brakes that pulled the craft around before it hit the ground. The pilot could focus entirely on his target as the plane approached its optimum bombing level of about

1,476ft. This was a new era of warfare and, initially, the Stuka proved a key part of Germany's success. The Stuka led other fast-moving forces against a dazed enemy.

Germans called it counter attack with pursuit. In the west, it was known as *Blitzkrieg*. Either way, it signalled a major new role for bombers in helping to drive forward tanks and infantry in a lightning assault. With this first employment of Blitzkrieg the Germans were eating away like predators at the carcass of Poland to the tune of 30–37 miles a day.

The architect of *Blitzkrieg* was Heinz Guderian, a German general inspired to change the way warfare was conducted after being stuck in the mud in Flanders during the First World War. The style of warfare that he created was intended to harrass the enemy constantly, giving soldiers no time to regroup. This is precisely what happened in Poland as German forces, entering the country on several fronts, drove defending troops into isolated pockets, whose resistance, no matter how fervent, was ultimately fruitless.

Poland had been reinstated as a nation after the First World War, having been a disputed territory since the eighteenth century. Long-held Polish national ambitions were finally recognised, but its territory divided Germany and East Prussia, some of which was ruled by Germany. Having reversed many facets of the treaty that ended the conflict already, it was no surprise that Hitler had Poland in his sights. There was also simmering unrest between resident Germans and Poles that provided a convenient excuse for an attack.

On the same day that the unannounced invasion by Germany began, the Prime Minister Neville Chamberlain spoke to Parliament, conceding that his previously held policy of appeasement had failed:

The time has come when action rather than speech is required ....

No man can say that the Government could have done more to try to keep open the way for an honourable and equitable settlement of the dispute between Germany and Poland. Nor have we neglected any means of making it crystal clear to the German Government that if they insisted on using force again in the manner in which they had used it in the past we were resolved to oppose them by force.

On 3 September, Britain declared war on Germany and five hours later France echoed the sentiment. At home, although there was no sign of imminent threat, there was a strong feeling that hostilities would be immediate and immense. In Coventry, a regular churchgoer, Beryl Ann Leadley, knew something was amiss when her father kept her in on the Sunday morning that war was declared for fear of something occurring.

That day, Betty Daniel had gone for a walk after church to rural Corley with John, the baby of the family. A woman came out of one of the cottages there shouting, 'You must get home now, war has been declared'. Anxiety was so heightened that some of her family had come looking for her on their bicycles. Everyone thought the Germans would attack immediately.

The more rational declared that Coventry was too far inland to be bombed. And at the time that Chamberlain made his announcement, when German fliers were restricted to German airfields, they might well have had a case. In her diary, Mary Bloomfield recalls a trip from Coventry following the declaration of war.

I caught the 2.15 pm bus from Pool Meadow and took my gas mask with me. I was surprised to see people behaving quite normally – all going about the business and enjoying Sunday in their usual manner.

Boys and girls were cycling off into the country taking their teas with them. Family parties set off in cars on the same errand. Children went for walks or to Sunday school. Some carried gas masks but not all.

The police carried their gas masks and steel helmets slung on their backs. There were quite a number of men in Army and Air Force uniforms about, a strange sight in Coventry.

She noted that the only indications the country was at war were the sight of windows swathed in blackout material or brown paper and cardboard, sandbags cladding important civic buildings and the fact that her policeman husband Ted was now working twelve-hour shifts:

The sun shone out of a clear blue sky. The balloon barrage was up and the aluminium painted sausages were a pleasing sight. The sun's rays picked them out, brilliant silver spots against the blue of the summer sky and below, bright green English meadows.

It seemed impossible that suddenly, out of that summer sky, death might come, heralded by sirens, hooters and the roaring of enemy aircraft engines [followed by] the crashing of bombs.

Yet that is what we are all prepared for, a sudden lightning raid to take us all by surprise. But it didn't come and the sun still shone when I reached Nuneaton.

Many towns emptied of men who joined the services. In Coventry, men were still abundant, as they were needed in the factories to make equipment for the armed forces and deemed to be in 'reserved occupations'. Indeed, skilled workers were being imported from other parts of the UK.

New laws were soon formulated to stop employees from changing jobs unless they had special permission from the Labour Exchange. Another existing Labour Act, restricting the length of the working day to eight hours, was suspended while the retirement age was raised from sixty-five to seventy.

If Britain's monumental declaration of war had an effect at home, it proved cold comfort to Poland. Just days later, its capital, Warsaw, was being pounded daily by German artillery, parked some 30 miles from the city's outskirts, and bomber squadrons fifty-strong. One man recollected the successive attacks:

> Graves were appearing everywhere. They multiplied quickly in front of churches, on malls and on squares. There was no way that you could get human remains to a cemetery. There were no caskets because the suppliers had run out. People were slapping together wooden boxes, or were simply wrapping what was left of the body in a sheet. I saw a grave with a fragment of a broken window frame serving as a cross.
>
> From the detonation of heavy ordnance the stucco cover of buildings peeled off like skin leaving the red flesh of bricks behind. Chimneys pointed upwards along with what was left of roofs and walls, staying up in spite of the laws of gravity, threatening to topple at any minute. The streets were covered with rubble forming barriers several stories high. The unbearable

fetid smell of burned objects and the dust from crushed concrete made it difficult to breathe.

Pianist Wladyslaw Szpilman was trapped in the city at the time and remembered the battle as it reached a crescendo:

> The dreadful days of 25 and 26 September came. The noise of explosions merged with the constant thunder of guns, penetrated by the boom of nose-diving aircraft like electric drills boring holes in iron. The air was heavy with smoke and the dust of crumbling bricks and plaster. It got everywhere, stifling people who had shut themselves up in cellars or their flats, keeping as far as possible from the street.
>
> How I survived those two days I do not know. A splinter of shrapnel killed someone sitting next to me in our friends' bedroom. I spent two nights and a day with ten people standing in a tiny lavatory. A few weeks later, when we wondered how it had been possible, and tried to squeeze ourselves in there again, we found that only eight people could possibly fit in unless they were in terror for their lives.

After eighteen days of perpetual bombardment and an invasion by Russian troops in the east, the Poles surrendered. There had been hopes in Warsaw that the French would mount a diversionary offensive against Germany in the west – a treaty existed between the two countries guaranteeing mutual support. However, French thinking was still dominated by the static warfare that had distinguished the First World War a generation earlier. Having built the Maginot Line, the French wanted to remain behind it to

defend France. The military was confident in the defensive
Maginot line that was built to withstand German aggression.
The fact that German troops did not immediately pour
through it was not a sign of its impregnability; rather, that
Hitler chose to bide his time in the winter months.

The British moved troops into France while Poland was
being pounded, but once again the importance of the
innovative new style of waging war seemed to pass them by as
they headed for what they believed to be a front line. For the
moment, it didn't matter. Germany had an easy victory in
Poland, while France and Britain felt themselves in full
command of the border.

Despite a surprise rebuff of his peace initiative, Hitler
pledged not to bomb Britain, and the British government
hesitated to target Germany for fear of reprisals. It was, after
all, much quicker for Luftwaffe planes to bomb London
from their northern airfields than for RAF bombers to reach
Berlin. In Britain, there were plenty of preparations for a
welter of expected aerial attacks. Air-raid shelters were hastily
built and mortuaries were stacked with cardboard coffins.
Each home was issued with a stirrup pump to douse fires and
a long-handled shovel to smother incendiaries with sand or
dirt. An uneasy calm descended over the country with the
winter months. For men of the British Expeditionary Force
in France and those at home, there began the so-called
'phoney' war. Winston Churchill called it the 'twilight' war,
while the Germans thought of it as '*Sitzkreig*', a sitting war.

The evacuation of children from areas considered at risk
to safe rural idylls began at the start of the conflict. For many
children, if it happened at all, it was a short-term arrangement
that ended when the promised rain of bombs failed to
materialise. In Coventry, an estimated twenty per cent of

those eligible were evacuated – one of the lowest figures among British cities – and most drifted back to the city within a matter of months. Betty Daniel was not evacuated, but nonetheless her life was changed by the onset of war.

A large underground shelter was built at Hen Lane School where she was a pupil. It was spacious enough for all the pupils, and two or three times a week there was a drill to see how quickly the children could all get inside after the sirens went. In common with every other pupil, she walked to school – in her case, a distance of almost two miles – wearing a blue T-shirt and grey pinafore dress, with grey knee-length socks which were all washed at weekends. At midday, she returned for lunch and then walked back for afternoon lessons. On the way, she would deliberately scuff her shoes – studded with nails by her father to make them last longer – to see sparks erupt from the sole. At home, her uncle, who was a builder, constructed a shelter for the family, which was set deeply into the garden with only a third of it visible above ground. It did not flood like others were prone to doing, so it was more comfortable than many.

The profile of family life changed, too. With dads, brothers and uncles in the forces, mums, aunties and sisters all went to work in the factories in their places. Ultimately, women were conscripted, too, and the era of the stay-at-home mother ended.

Betty's after-school chores included putting water buckets around the house in case of a fire following a raid and placing the stirrup pump by the tap. There were also sand buckets on hand to put out incendiary devices. When she settled in for the evening, she used to knit items for servicemen. Her favourite was to make a sea boot for sailors in cream wool and on average she produced one every night.

Some things did not change: the family still used the old metal bath and shared the water, with Betty going first, followed by her brother, mother and father. The laundry was still done outside in the yard in a big 'copper' – something similar to a cauldron with a space for fire underneath – and clothes were changed just once a week. Newspaper threaded on string was used instead of toilet paper.

If there were food shortages, it was not immediately apparent to Betty. She usually had porridge for breakfast, although sometimes there was toast and eggs. The main meal of the day, served at lunchtime and called dinner, was usually something from a stew pot. It might have been short on meat, but there were plenty of vegetables. At tea time, there were sandwiches with either lard or dripping – or sometimes jam. On Sunday, teas would comprise home-grown fruit, sometimes with cream, and bread and butter. Vegetables were home grown; abundant in the summer and salted for the spare months of the rest of the year. Fruit was available if it was in season. The glut was preserved in Kilner jars to last through the winter. Presents at birthdays and Christmases for Betty meant some knitting wool and, once, a knitting bag, a penny, an apple, orange and some nuts. One uncle used to bring a clockwork toy.

Early in the war, advice was published in one of the factory magazines on what to buy a schoolgirl: a propelling pencil, a well-fitted pencil box, or a pixie hood and scarf to match. For schoolboys, a torch, fountain pen, stamp album and small attaché case were recommended. The suggested items for servicemen were gloves or mittens, a warm cardigan, slippers, some playing cards, a writing case, a new razor and blade, books, toffees, a reliable fountain pen, a propelling pencil and a travelling ink container.

Sports-mad Betty and her friends were used to an outdoor life full of physical activity. They made matchstick boats and sailed them in a local brook. With the advent of war, Livingstone Road Baths and Coventry Swimming Baths were closed and turned into first-aid centres, so for five years no children were taught to swim. Undeterred, Betty and others hitched a ride on the coal lorry to Nuneaton, where they would swim outdoors in a pond.

There were risks attached to this kind of childhood freedom. Betty's brother, Robert Challoner died in 1938, aged fifteen. He had suffered a devastating spine injury after falling from a stile when he was eight years old. Every night, her father dressed the injury. However, seven years later, tuberculosis set in and it killed him. A family holiday arranged shortly after his death took the remainder of the Challoner family to Colwyn Bay and it was the first time Betty had seen the sea.

British people were urged to 'put that light out', 'dig for victory', buy war bonds, carry their gas masks, know that careless talk cost lives and to 'keep calm and carry on'. For those who did not instantly take this advice, there was a raft of legislation to make it the norm. Emergency laws were so sweeping that one Member of Parliament complained that the British people were fighting Nazi aggression abroad and Nazi tendencies at home. Largely, though, people complied with the flurry of Whitehall notices, although, with a national blackout imposed by the government, the number of road accidents soared until low lighting was finally permitted. It was impossible to discern pedestrians in the blackout, according to Mary Bloomfield, unless they were smoking and the red tip of their cigarette offered a vital clue to their whereabouts, plus 'cyclists were difficult to see. They just seemed to loom up in the dark, a black shape against the faint glow of the headlights.'

At work, other measures were being instituted to safeguard employees and the local economy from aerial threat. Factories built systems of walls and doors to shield the glare of their furnaces – although many people were uncomfortably aware that German dignitaries had toured Coventry factories in the years leading up to war and the precise position of established premises was well known.

With such success in the art of persuasion at home, it was not surprising that the British government chose not to drop bombs on the German people in the opening weeks of the war, but instead to shower them with a multitude of messages, too. It was a technique used in the First World War, urging German soldiers in the trenches to hand themselves over to the British. This time, the leaflets asked for the German people to 'insist on peace'. On the first day of the war, six million pamphlets cascaded down on what must have been bemused populaces in Hamburg, Bremen and nine cities in the Ruhr. This followed a statement from both the French and British governments promising to avoid bombing civilians and making it clear that they had no intention of resorting to poisonous gas or germ warfare. Dubbed 'the confetti war', the propaganda drops continued, amply serving to show the Germans where they needed to beef up anti-aircraft gun emplacements. One popular story at the time told of a squadron leader admonishing a flying officer for not untying a bundle of leaflets before sending them out of the plane: 'Lord, man, you might have hurt someone!'

Josef Goebbels was unimpressed. 'If the British aeroplanes fly at tremendous heights at night and drop their ridiculous propaganda in German territory, I have nothing against it,' said the Nazi Propaganda Minister. 'But take care if the leaflets are replaced by one bomb. Then reprisals will follow as in Poland.' The Germans did not bomb the British that winter.

Giving a speech in Manchester on 27 January 1940, Winston Churchill – not yet Prime Minister – frankly admitted he could not explain the lack of German air raiders although it was not from 'any false sense of delicacy that they have so far refrained from subjecting us to this new and odious form of attack.

'But for the present, here is a chapter of war which they have not chosen to open upon us because they cannot tell what may be written in its final pages.'

He went on to back the 'confetti' method of warfare, as it gave an unready Britain more time to prepare: 'Not only have our air defences and shelters been markedly improved, but our armies at home and abroad, which are now very large, are steadily maturing in training and in quality, and the whole preparation of our munitions industries under the spur of war has rolled forward with gathering momentum'.

Such was the hesitancy to use aerial weaponry that the Secretary of State for Air, Sir Howard Kingsley Wood, refused to permit the bombing of the Black Forest in September 1939 on the grounds that it was private property.

Still, this 'softly, softly' approach was a cause of enormous consternation to some who were uncomfortable in the knowledge that what happened in Poland was likely to occur elsewhere. An anonymous letter to the *Sunday Times* in January 1940 asked why there were no air strikes against Germany when there was no prospect of a land-based attack and any victory by sea would be a long, drawn-out affair.

Leaflets were still being dropped in February, but by now the range was greater. Using French airfields, British aeroplanes could reach Prague, Vienna and Warsaw. The following month, a frustrated Lord Trenchard – a founder of the Royal Air Force – felt impelled to remind the House of Lords that by nature its aircraft were offensive, rather than defensive. Less than two months after that, he urged more strongly for a change of tack:

> If it is wrong for me to say that I should like to see military objectives in Germany hit by air, it is a thousand times more wrong for the Government to help the Germans by saying that we shall never do it ....
>
> Make no mistake about it: when the time comes, Germany will hit us by air, over towns and military objectives alike, mercilessly and thoroughly. Why should we await her convenience before striking at military targets in Germany?

Still, hospital beds were empty and lime pits that had been prepared for mutilated corpses remained unfilled. And still there was limited action by the Royal Air Force and a virtual no-show over England by the Luftwaffe.

Even without the exhortation by President Roosevelt about restraint when it came to bombing, British aeroplanes would have had a task on their hands if they wanted to attack German cities. Holland and Belgium remained neutral and did not take kindly to British aircraft taking a short-cut through their air space. It meant a long dog-leg detour for the British aircraft just to reach northern German cities and thus put them on the outer limits of their range.

Systems for civil defence which had been put into place in Coventry at the start of the war, whereby the city was divided into six areas, each with a zone controller, remained untested. That winter, Coventry was once again focused more on the IRA than Nazi Germany, as the trial of two men linked to the killings the previous August unfolded.

Irishman Peter Barnes had been arrested in London on the same day as the Coventry blast in connection with a planned bicycle bombing campaign in the capital. He had returned to the capital after delivering the necessary explosives to 25 Clara Street, the home of the Hewitt family from Northern Ireland, who had moved to Coventry to seek work. The man who collected the new bicycle that was later loaded with a bomb and left in Broadgate was the family's lodger, James McCormick. However, the person responsible for building the bomb and parking the bicycle was never identified.

At a trial held in Warwick in December 1939, thirty-two-year-old Barnes and McCormick, who was twenty-nine, were found guilty of murder. Although McCormick acknowledged his guilt, Barnes continued to protest his innocence until the last. The Hewitts, who ran the safe house, were acquitted of the killings but deported back to Belfast. Numerous pleas for clemency were ignored. In one letter to the government, Britain's leading Roman Catholic, the Archbishop of Westminster, Cardinal Arthur Hinsley, promised to renew 'in the strongest terms' the condemnation of the 'cowardly methods' of the IRA, saying he was confident that the denunciation of the group would be stronger in Ireland if the sentences were commuted: 'If the immediate commutation of the sentence cannot be granted it is suggested that the death penalty be delayed with the threat that it would be carried out at once on the recurrence of any further IRA outrages.'

But there was no sign that the British government was about to consider clemency, no matter how much that might improve rocky relations between the two countries.

Éamon de Valera, the Taoiseach of the Republic of Ireland, wrote to Prime Minister Neville Chamberlain saying

> The reprieve of these men would be regarded as an act of generosity which would be a thousand times more valuable to Britain than anything that could possibly be gained by their death. The latter will be looked upon as an act fitting only too sadly into the historic background of our relations. Almost superhuman patience is required on both sides to exorcise feelings which the knowledge of centuries have engendered.'

On the following day, 6 February 1940, de Valera wrote to King George VI, acknowledging that the case fell entirely within the jurisdiction of the British government but once again warning of the damage the executions of the IRA members would do to the relationship between the UK and the Republic at a time when, he claimed, links were 'steadily improving'. Repercussions might affect the way Ireland's neutrality in the war was conducted and, he said, cause a backlash in the United States as well as in Ireland.

Tom Barry, the leader of the IRA in Cork, also secretly contacted the British government via de Valera, asking for a four-day stay of execution to 'put conclusive proof' before the Home Secretary that neither Barnes nor McCormick conspired in or had knowledge of the Coventry explosion. None of the entreaties was successful. As expected, their hangings at Winson Green Prison in Birmingham on 7 February 1940, which was Ash Wednesday, caused widespread fury in Ireland, where it was pointed out that neither of the executed men took part in the final leg of the outrage. It was claimed that the bicycle should have been left at the electricity substation, the kind of facility that was often targeted at the time. No one knows why the bicycle with its deadly cargo was left in a busy shopping centre. Outraged Republicans festered with the desire for revenge. In reality, there would be nothing the IRA could do by way of retaliation that would match the strikes later inflicted by Nazi Germany. Although it did not end the IRA campaign, the Coventry bomb did cast a long shadow over it, with its Irish architect later branding the S-plan 'a damp and inglorious squib'.

With the IRA executions, one chapter of Coventry's history appeared to close, while another seemed set to begin. But in the early months of 1940, it was still the blackout rather than bombers that was causing the greatest difficulty for people. With no street lighting, there was a fear that men would lurk to pounce on the unwary, and it was not entirely unjustified. Beryl Ann Leadley was a young teenager who had recently joined the youth club when she was approached as she walked home in darkness at 9.00 p.m..

From behind, she suddenly heard a gruff voice asking, 'What would you do for a naughty man for a good price?'. Without stopping to answer, she raced home.

Meanwhile, RAF Bomber Command was far from idle, but highly selective in choosing targets. A large part of the army was poised but inactive in France.

With wintry weather less conducive to aerial operations, war at this time was being waged at sea where there was less opportunity for, or inclination towards, restraint. The war at sea had continued much as it had started with the Glasgow-registered liner *Athenia* being sunk by a U-boat with the loss of 112 lives on the day war was declared. One of the most notable naval disasters occurred a month later when the battleship *Royal Oak* was sunk after a U-boat penetrated the naval base at Scapa Flow, leaving 800 dead. Shipping losses continued to mount during 1940 and British hopes of conducting an effective blockade of German ports faltered.

British aeroplanes continued to do sweeps of coastal waters, occasionally catching U-boats on the surface. There were also repeated raids at Sylt against German seaplanes which had been responsible for mining British waters. The perils of daylight raids and close formation flying became starkly apparent during this period, with the RAF sustaining surprisingly heavy losses. Although British troops were still in Europe, it seemed Germany retained the upper hand.

## Chapter Four

# 'Calling all workers'

*Theme tune to the BBC's*
Music While You Work *Radio Programme*

For some, the phoney war ended with the invasion of Denmark and Norway on 9 April 1940, although the response of the RAF was still restrained. Unable to support British and French incursions in the north of Norway for lack of range, RAF aeroplanes were compelled to bomb the southern part of the country. There was also a long-standing policy in place to conserve aeroplanes rather than risk them in uncertain operations. Indeed, the overall British reaction was noticeably hesitant and haphazard, while Germany's command of the air proved far more useful than Britain's sea supremacy. A Parliamentary debate soon afterwards about the ineffective Allied intervention in Norway led to the resignation of Neville Chamberlain, and Winston Churchill replacing him.

In the *Daily Mail* of 26 April 1940, the veteran Conservative Alfred Duff Cooper returned to the theme of the quiet air war when he wrote: 'There would appear to exist a kind of unwritten truce between the great belligerents according to the tacit terms of which they do not bomb one another but are all agreed upon the bombing of smaller countries.'

Within two weeks, any semblance of a 'truce' evaporated after German troops flooded into the Low Countries, heading for France. An about-turn on British policy governing aerial bombardments was made after Rotterdam, the throbbing commercial centre of the Netherlands, was flattened by a concerted Luftwaffe attack at lunchtime on 14 May 1940. By teatime, the Dutch government had surrendered. Thankfully, reports of some 30,000 casualties in the attack were grossly exaggerated, but nearly 1,000 people died and the medieval heart of the city was left smouldering for days.

Within twenty-four hours, the British War Cabinet began targeting German oil and communications industries and dispatched ninety-nine bombers on a raid on the Ruhr under the cover of darkness, in full recognition that civilians were being put at risk.

It did little to thwart the *Blitzkrieg* in northern Europe, however. Without stopping at the Belgian border, German forces swept into France and encircled retreating British troops in its northeast corner. With the evacuation of British troops at Dunkirk – more than 338,000 were taken off the beaches by a range of craft – and the swift fall of France, the phoney war was officially at an end.

Those who had stayed at their posts in the factories now heard of former colleagues who had perished on the beaches at Dunkirk. The Royal Warwickshire Regiment had a strong presence in the British Expeditionary Force that was chased out of France in May and June. Private John Casey of the Royal Warwickshire Regiment, who had formerly worked in the Alfred Herbert factory's milling department, died in Belgium on 31 May. Although it is likely he perished on the beaches, forty-five men from his regiment were massacred four days earlier at Wormhoudt after being captured by an SS unit.

Maurice Cole, a miner's son from Bedworth serving as a Regiment Signaller with 1/7 Battalion, staged a brave last stand against the advancing German army in May 1940, as Operation Dynamo, the code name for the evacuation of British troops, was in full swing. The former Armstrong Siddeley engineer was on foot when he was captured amid the chaos of the Dunkirk retreat. After being interrogated, Maurice was marched across Holland to Germany and transported to Stalag 1Xc camp, where he was forced to work in the salt mines for the remainder of the war. Although Maurice was posted as 'missing, presumed dead', his details were taken by the Dutch Red Cross and his family back in Bedworth was subsequently informed that he was a prisoner.

Reg Brown, from Bedworth, was with the Royal Engineers when he boarded the SS *Lancastria* at St Nazaire two weeks after Dunkirk as frantic efforts to retrieve remaining British forces still stranded in France continued. The ship – overcrowded with soldiers and refugees – was blown up when a Luftwaffe bomb slithered down one of its funnels and it sank swiftly with an estimated loss of 7,500 souls. Although he survived, Reg became a prisoner of war.

Later, he recalled how he heard a woman refugee screaming for someone to save her baby while he was in the water: 'One of my mates swam over and used his teeth to keep the little one afloat. [Years later] I was at a remembrance service when a lady came up to me and said she was that very same baby.'

The *Lancastria* tragedy was kept secret by the British government for fear of further denting public morale following Dunkirk. Even without news of the disaster, there must have been enough happening to persuade workers on the home front in Coventry that they were in the right place so far as personal safety was concerned. With the majority of the British Army's guns and trucks abandoned in France, the ambitious task of Coventry's factory workers was now clearly defined. The country had to be equipped with military hardware – and fast.

Many manufacturers operated more than one site in the city. Rover and Standard employees were spread across three factories while Armstrong, Whitworth, Daimler, Morris and Sterling Metals had two. Days in the factories were long and hard, but there was some light relief from 23 June onwards when *Music While You Work* was broadcast by the BBC in two half-hour slots. Both programmes began with a rousing trumpet summons, the start of the theme tune by Eric Coates known as 'Calling All Workers'. There were guidelines about the type of music played: fast music was deemed 'unsettling' while slow tunes were soporific. It also had to be heard through the hubbub of a factory, so complicated melodies were unsuitable. Military bands were popular choices and BBC executives believed that production increased by 13 per cent when the programme was broadcast.

But defeat for the Allies in Western Europe wrought other changes that would have a direct bearing not only on British workers but also on their families. As the battle for France ended, so the battle of Britain began and now every industrial centre in the country was in range of the Luftwaffe. The notion that Coventry was safe from Hitler's bombers was no longer true. Yet the city was not unprepared. Coventry's fire brigade was poised and ready: twenty Auxiliary Fire Brigade stations were spread around the outskirts, and there were a growing number of works brigades and forty fire patrols. There were also several detachments of the Home Guard, some of which were based at city factories, as well as anti-aircraft emplacements, pillboxes, first-aid volunteers and a small battalion of wardens. And it was just as well, as it was only a matter of time before Britain started suffering under a bombing campaign, with supremacy of the skies being the precursor to an invasion that Hitler now planned.

In retrospect, a decision to fudge requests by the doomed French government in its dying days for extra air resources from Britain seems justified, the French having decided to save Paris from aerial assault by declaring it an open city. Still, even with that economy made, on paper everything seemed to be in Germany's favour. The Luftwaffe had fine machines in which to fly, newly acquired airfields in Normandy and a stock of brave and experienced pilots, and their stocks of oil had been replenished by those of Poland.

Against this formidable enemy stood mostly untested young pilots who were nonetheless fired up at the thought of repelling the first invasion of Britain since 1066.

By the middle of August, the battle began in earnest. Still, the primary targets chosen by the Luftwaffe and by the RAF were military ones. However, on 23 August, during an attack on a Thameside oil installation, some stray bombs killed civilians in London.

Churchill's reprisal was swift and exacting. Eighty-one Hampden bombers from two squadrons carried out a bombing raid on Berlin. Cloud cover made the targeting wildly inaccurate, so it caused minimal disruption in which only six people died. Still, Luftwaffe chief Hermann Göring was embarrassed and Hitler was furious that his prized capital city could be bombed. In a speech, he promised to reply in kind, and the following month a series of concerted attacks on London took place. For the first time, Britain experienced the terrors of the Blitz, with its civilians in the front line.

It began on 7 September, later dubbed 'Black Saturday'. That night 348 bombers, escorted by 617 fighters, droned over London dropping thousands of pounds of explosives. Nearly 450 people died. Nor was London's Blitz confined to a single night; the raids continued in earnest for two months, with no respite. The American journalist Ed Murrow told the free world in radio reports how Britain was defending itself: 'Decisive battles of history are being fought by a few, high in the blue sky ....

'At dawn Londoners come oozing out of the ground, tired and red eyed and sleepy. The fires are dying down. I saw them turn into their own street to see if their house was still standing.'

He spoke of a beleaguered people's courage, the flash and roar of the ack-ack guns rolling down the streets and the stench of the air-raid shelters where women and children crouched in terror through long blast-ridden nights. And he was not the only broadcaster to sense that civilians were for the first time in the front line. The novelist and playwright J. B. Priestly took to the airwaves to laud the stoicism of the nation's targeted population:

> We see now, when the enemy bombers come roaring at us at all hours, and it's our nerve versus his, that we're not really civilians any longer but a mixed lot of soldiers – machine-minding soldiers, milkmen and postmen soldiers, housewives and mother soldiers – and what a gallant corps that is – even broadcasting soldiers. Now and then, we ought to be paraded, and perhaps a few medals handed out.

Later, medals were indeed handed out to the servicemen who helped defend the country, and there were a few for exceptional acts among the rest of the population. Yet, most nights brought forth a raft of small heroic gestures that went without public recognition or acclaim. London was not the only city to be hard hit. Liverpool – an obvious target because of its docks – was being heavily bombed and towns in the Midlands, where industry was racing to re-arm, were experiencing an escalating number of raids by the Luftwaffe.

Despite the repeated attacks, none of the cities was brought to its knees. London covered a large area. No amount of pounding, it seemed, would make the capital capitulate. Eventually, the penny dropped with Luftwaffe's High Command. Concentrated firepower in much smaller areas would have more far-reaching consequences. Thus, Coventry emerged as a front-runner among possible targets. It was already being bombed on a small scale.

The city's first air raid occurred on 14 August 1940 when bombs fell in the Cannon Park Road area. There were no casualties, but any misplaced belief that the city would be saved from Luftwaffe attentions was rudely dispelled. For most people, it was now a case of 'when' and not 'if' the Germans invaded and it brought about changes to their daily routines.

People carried gas masks – or at least they were supposed to – and even bus companies painted out their vehicles' windows so that they would not be detected from the air at night.

Women bore the brunt of this home front upheaval. There were queues at shops, a shortage of fresh food and husbands away from home, either at work or in the services. From 1941, young women were compelled to register for work but many joined the war effort before that. And it was not just the young, single women who ended up working in the factories – often young mothers volunteered to work as well. To help those women who wanted to work, but who had young children at home, the government established a National Childcare Scheme, building nurseries where parents could leave youngsters while they went to work. Children would be cared for all day and receive their meals at the cost of one shilling per day.

A letter from a Mrs J.L. Jones to the *Midlands Daily Telegraph* on 24 August 1940 underlined how important these nurseries were for local families.

> The problem of providing nurseries is urgent ... Many hundreds of women with children are now working in Coventry's factories; their children need to be properly cared for. Many hundreds more women would rally to the appeal made daily in your advertisement columns for women to undertake national work – if they were sure that their children would be looked after properly by trained people while they were at work.

Childcare was not the only thing on the minds of the city's young mothers at the time. Many believed invading troops intent on fostering Nazism would be capable of savage behaviour, which put them in danger. There were fears expressed among Coventry women that they would be shipped out to 'baby farms' in Germany after an invasion. Some wanted a pile of hand grenades in their bedrooms to slaughter Germans as they made their way up Coventry streets. In her diary, Mary Bloomfield admitted that she was considering putting powerful weed-killer in her kettle, then offering the invaders a cup of tea.

The sound of the air-raid siren was becoming a common feature of Coventry life even though London was still the primary target of the Luftwaffe. The siren, either electrically operated or hand-cranked, was at a pitch especially designed to be heard through brick walls. But even if the siren sounded, it did not mean there was going to be a full-blown raid. Sometimes, it was a lone aircraft flying high above the city, probably on a reconnaissance mission. At worst, bombs were dropped by low-flying planes – and already the number of casualties was mounting.

Secretary Christina Stephenson experienced a 'near miss' early in the aerial war.

She had been caught outside in a short, sharp August raid and recalled how the sound of the bomb falling at close quarters seemed like a hurricane. A tide of panic washed over her in tandem with the roar of the bomb. Her heart told her to run the few yards between the street and home but she resisted the temptation, certain that the house was about to be blown off its foundations. As she clamped her hands over her ears, she saw the bomb whistle over the roof of her house and head into the city beyond.

It landed on the 2,500 seater Rex Cinema, which had been opened two years previously in Corporation Street with some ceremony. A fine example of the Art Deco style, its smooth lines were about as far from the description of 'flea pit' as it was possible to get. Now the stylish cinema was consigned to the pages of history. Certainly, the admired Wurlitzer organ would never sound a chord again.

In a quirk of fate that Coventry folk recalled for years afterwards, the cinema had been due on the following night to show with a showing of *Gone with the Wind* for the first time. Fans might justifiably have felt disappointed at losing the opportunity to see the long-awaited Hollywood film of the Margaret Mitchell novel with Clark Gable and Vivien

Leigh which had been wowing crowds elsewhere. Instead, they were simply relieved that the cinema was empty when the roof fell in. Besides, the Rex did not stand alone as a picture house in Coventry. Its destruction left no fewer than twenty-two cinemas open for business, reflecting how popular this form of entertainment was at the time.

Christina Stephenson worked at Daimler in Radford where her job as secretary to the cashier included filling sixty brown envelopes with wages each work for fellow workers. Meticulously, she counted out coppers including fiddly farthings and piles of silver coins like shillings, florins and half crowns. Usually, the crumpled, brown ten-shilling notes had to be smoothed into shape before being placed inside the envelopes. Green pound notes were common enough, too, although Christina never had a £5 note at her finger tips. Even though Daimler workers considered themselves well off, none of those on the factory floor earned more than £5 a week – and some got considerably less.

It was not her first job: Christina had begun her working life at Coventry Bicycles some five years previously. Like most girls, she finished school at the age of fourteen, in 1933. But unlike many of her playground pals, she went on to take shorthand lessons with a private tutor and mastered the outlines of the Pitman system in preparation for office life. She also learned typing and book keeping. With qualifications like that and the buoyant economy in Coventry, she could take her pick of jobs. Plenty of people enjoyed the same freedom and flexibility at the time, leaving work with one company on Friday and joining another the following Monday morning.

At Daimler, Christina met the man who would become her husband, Leonard, and they started dating in 1935 after meeting by chance on the concourse outside the Daimler factory, where Len was chief metallurgist dealing with electroplating and the heat treatment processes necessary in car production. Coventry's proud history in the motor industry had begun at Daimler at the end of the nineteenth century.

At the time of their first encounter, Len was courting Rhoda, a brunette, who was already talking about marriage. Uncertain, Len had sidestepped the subject every time it came up. When he met Christina that day, he suddenly realised why. The attraction was immediate and mutual. Perhaps realising the hopelessness of her situation, Rhoda soon ran off with Len's family's lodger.

Christina thought that Len had the looks of a film star, and the actor who came to mind was Allan Jones, best known as the star of the 1936 musical *Show Boat*, and the father of singer Jack Jones, who was born two years later.

Christina and Len used to see each other six nights out of seven. Before the war, they were content with a walk around the neighbourhood followed by sandwiches – ham, corned beef or cheese – delivered to them in the tidy front room of her family home. They also went to the cinema as often as they could. But as the number of raids increased in Coventry, the options for courting couples like Christina and Len narrowed. With autumn approaching, the reality of war became ever more apparent.

As if to prove it, in September, the 95th Anti Aircraft Royal Artillery came to Coventry from Scapa Flow, basing itself at a gun site opposite Binley Colliery, bringing more soldiers onto the streets. The new arrivals found the emplacement spacious with four 3.7-inch guns surrounded by sandbags and storage space for a large quantity of shells. Inside the concrete command post were three key instruments, the spotter, a Czechoslovakian-made height and range finder – considered one of the finest in the world – and a predictor. For the first time the men encountered a new system of tracking enemy planes known as radar or, sometimes, radio location. The hut it was in was surrounded by a taut carpet of wire netting with a radius of some 30 yds and supported on stakes about 4 ft from the ground in order to improve the accuracy of the radar beam.

Even before the Blitz the men of the unit were called out on a nightly basis. After an evening meal at 5.00 p.m., they would retire to their huts in full operational gear – including a great coat, leather jerkin and respirator – and lie on their beds with tin helmets by their side waiting for the sound of the siren, and most evenings, they were not lying down for long.

Coventry lacked the Underground's tunnels that provided shelter for hundreds during the London Blitz or the deep shelters that protected the German population, but there were sizeable public surface shelters as well as domestic Anderson shelters for those who had had sufficient foresight to install them. However, the general consensus was that the shelters were rather unsavoury places and the difficulties associated with the accommodation offered by shelters in Coventry and elsewhere was discussed in a government report:

The problem of night sleeping in shelters is the greatest concern of observers, particularly in the poor and crowded districts. Sanitary arrangements in many cases are inadequate: the atmosphere becomes very foul: there are increasing numbers of cases of colds and septic throats especially among children and it is feared that there may be epidemics. In several districts cases of blatant immorality in shelters are reported;

this upsets other occupants of shelters and will deter
them from using the shelters again.

But the options were few. When the klaxon moaned, most
people headed for the shelters as if they were on autopilot.
Occasionally, however, some would question whether they
would be safer inside the shelter or outside. It was certainly
pleasanter to remain at home rather than trudging to the
shelter where most people smoked. Furthermore, the lavatory
was often no more than a bucket screened off by a curtain.
Some had benches with holes in the seats and a bucket beneath.
When people were scared, the bucket filled even more quickly
than usual and this all contributed to a choking atmosphere.

In wet weather, water seeped up through the duck boards
that lined the base of the shelter. It was cold and yet still
stuffy, with the only warmth coming from hot water bottles,
heated house bricks wrapped in blankets or perhaps a candle
sheltered in an upturned terracotta pot. Babies cried in fear
or discomfort after they were installed for the night. Small
children would beg their parents to return to the warm beds
they had abandoned at the sound of the siren, especially in
the summer months when zealous ARP wardens announced
the presence of enemy aircraft without knowing where the
target would be. Inevitably, there was little time to make a
decision about whether to use the shelter or not and most
people shrugged as they crouched to enter through the low
doors, subscribing to the view that it was 'pot luck' whether
they would die there.

Thus streams of neighbours regularly made their way into
public and private shelters to sacrifice comfort for safety.

In the early hours of the morning, everyone uncurled
their limbs at the sound of the 'all clear', after being painfully

confined in the cold and damp, hunched with numerous others. Their hair was limp, their faces were lined with weariness. But there was no question of taking a day off work. Bosses in companies all over Coventry were very strict about attendance, despite the volley of disrupted nights.

Inexorably, the city's death toll was rising. On 12 October 1940, three members of the Logan family died when their home in Henry Street took a direct hit. For father Michael, mother Florence and five-year-old Frankie, there was no hope. But three rescuers – Albert Fearn, Frederick Mason and Thomas Lee – dug into the ruins, despite the risk posed by a fractured gas main. Together, they hauled six-and-a-half-year-old Michael Logan from the wreckage. His older brother, Patrick, was also saved.

It was the start of a distinguished civilian war-time service for Albert Fearn, who was later awarded the George Medal and Defence Medal. Fifty-five years later, Michael Logan bought the medals for £2,850 – his life savings – at auction to ensure that they were kept in Coventry. He loaned them to the city's Herbert Gallery for public display, his personal tribute to the man who saved his life. Sadly, the pair never met, as Albert died before Michael tracked him down. By coincidence, both men worked at the same time at the Massey Ferguson plant in Coventry without realising the other was there.

Also on 12 October, Stirling Metals, which made aluminium alloy products for the aero industry, and the Daimler Works were damaged. The same Daimler works was hit again two nights later. And on 16 October, when the raids in the Midlands were intensifying still further, there was more disruption and devastation. Despite her misgivings, Christina Stephenson had used a public shelter to escape the bombardment, which that night seemed aimed at her neighbourhood. Inside, she witnessed a scene that remained with her for the rest of her life. The door of the shelter opened as the muffled symphony of earth-shaking bombs drew to a close and, softly, a man called one of the women inside by name. Although she initially acknowledged him, the woman refused to move after seeing the expression on his face. While he urged her to come outside she kept her eyes ahead, choosing to ignore his pleadings. Everyone in the shelter was silent, waiting to see what would happen next. With a sigh, the pale face at the door eventually withdrew into the darkness.

The following morning the fears of all those inside the shelter – especially the unco-operative woman – were realised. Just a few hundred yards from it the Ford's Hospital, built as Alms Houses in 1509, lay in smoking ruins. No doubt one of the blasts that had shaken the shelter had scored a direct hit on the hospital that housed elderly women. Among the eight dead was Matron Florence Yates, the sister of the man who had been at the shelter door and of the woman who remained in the shelter. It was this dreadful news that the woman who had stayed put already knew, somewhere in her heart, without needing to be told.

The same night, a German aeroplane flew into a barrage balloon in Coventry, which brought the aircraft down and killed three of its four crew.

It was about this time that Mary Dale became a playground hero by taking an incendiary into school. To find an undetonated explosive like this was rare. Her father, an ARP warden, discovered it in the Butts shortly before the Blitz and took it home to show his family. When he dismantled, it he found sand in the base instead of any volatile substance, probably put there in a small act of sabotage by one of the slave labourers working in German factories to supply the Nazi war machine, risking death to do so. Watched closely by his daughter, he put the harmless weapon back together again and, the following day, he let her take it to school.

Mary was proud to produce such a show-stopping item in the classroom, but sadly, the headmistress did not share her enthusiasm. The appalled woman immediately summoned a senior official in the Civil Defence who promptly buried the incendiary in the school garden.

'I went home at dinner time, very upset, and my father who came home too at that time was very annoyed when I told him what had happened,' said Mary, who later shared her memories with Coventry's Herbert Museum.

'"Do they think I would let a child of mine take anything dangerous into school," he said. "'I'll take a spade and dig it up myself." And so he did.'

Escalating raids were having an increased effect on everyone's lives. For a long while, Christina felt lucky that her boyfriend was exempt from military service thanks to his important role in the factory. Later though, she wondered just how lucky she really was. When she emerged from the shelter, she had no idea where Len was or whether he was alive. It was the same for him, of course. It was not until she got to work that she knew for certain that Len had escaped the worst of the bombing. His family home was in Holbrooks, further from the centre than her own home.

From the outbreak of hostilities, the Daimler factory began making four-wheel-drive Scout cars for the Army, as well as armoured cars and parts to keep the war effort grinding on. Before he left the factory at night, Len filled his car with fuel. He had chosen to drive an open-top BSA three-wheeler with black and red livery because it was economical to run. Even so, rationing made petrol hard to come by, but fortunately, as a metallurgist, Len had good knowledge of chemistry and he could brew a concoction that would power it just as well after he had used his allocated petrol ration.

Behind her neighbours' closed doors, there was a frisson of panic whenever Len roared up to collect Christina. Windows shook in their frames and floorboards vibrated. As the engine noise intensified, residents wondered if a German aeroplane had sneaked into British airspace before there was time to sound the sirens. Those who glanced out of the window to assess the risks sighed with a mixture of relief and irritation when they saw the pint-sized car with the number plate FW9 039 which sounded as if it was propelled by jet engines. When he left at the end of the evening, the sound of the car took many minutes rather than seconds to recede into the distance.

The rising moan of the air-raid siren brought a small battalion of voluntary ambulance drivers and their assistants to Coventry and Warwickshire hospital, among them was twenty-year-old John Sargent. At the start of the war, it was agreed that St John Ambulance Brigade volunteers like John would do war work as an independent unit that was allied to the public authorities and the emergency medical services. The duties of the St John's men and women involved ambulance transport, stretcher bearing, hospital clearances and night duty in large basement air raid shelters, and the brigade had a representative on each ward of the hospital during an alert.

A well-practised drill to protect patients from injury during German attacks swung smoothly into action after the sound of the siren. Time was short and conversation was restricted to the bare essentials. Everyone knew what he or she had to do. As usual, John teamed up with colleague Doug Henderson to bring the most severely ill patients on stretchers down flights of stairs from the upper floors of the hospital to ground level. These patients – only recently out of the eye operating theatre – had to be kept flat. On the ground floor, the stretchers were slid under beds to provide protection from flying glass and masonry if a bomb was dropped. It was hard work, especially on the arms, and made hotter and more difficult by the cumbersome navy blue Civil Defence uniforms made from serge cotton. When the most vulnerable patients were safe, John and Doug went from ward to ward, talking to patients and keeping them calm. 'Don't worry,' they soothed. 'The hospital roof is covered with a giant red cross. No one is going to target this building.'

Until November 1940, the Germans specialised in nuisance raids, or *Storangriffe* as they termed them, which caused no greater nuisance than at the hospital where patients had to be put out of harm's way even when a bomb strike was apparently unlikely, and no one knew how long it would last. At the sound of the All Clear, the patients were carried back upstairs. It meant another night with little or no sleep for John, but he was used to it by now.

During the day, he worked at Modern Machine Tools, a Coventry factory, founded in 1928 by a businessman called Harry Weston, that made pumps and lathes. At the end of his shift, John headed for the ambulance station near the hospital where he stayed for twelve hours. There were three teams on call at night, working in rotation. The aim was to get some sleep in the station's bunk beds when other teams were in action.

But on a busy night, all three teams were likely to be called on to help with hospital patients. Sleep, food and other home comforts simply went by the board.

None of this worried John. He had been used to hard work since boyhood, when he was expected to help out at the rural water mill run by his father. And if he did not carry out his chores in a timely fashion, he could expect a clip around the ear. His father had once been a sheep farmer in Argentina, but had returned during the First World War when his own widowed father was ill, securing a job at a munitions factory in Newbury, in Berkshire. At his father's house, he fell in love with Alice, the housekeeper, and despite a substantial age difference they married and moved to a mill in nearby Hungerford. But money became tight, as village mills were bypassed in favour of large new steam-driven mills in towns and cities. Occasionally, the Sargents' mill would crank into action to provide some local housewives with flour or to grind barley for cattle. With the wheels in motion, the entire building shook. But the call for its services became increasingly rare and, with its timbers stilled by lack of demand, the family lived off the land. Young John had to tend vegetables, care for the hens and the ferrets used for catching rabbits, pick over potatoes stored over the winter and load up barrels of of them, which were sold for sixpence. Although the family was poor, John never went hungry like the children in the towns did during the slump of the Twenties and Thirties. However, when he was twelve, his life was turned upside down after his father died of a heart attack. His mother struggled to find work and finally decided to move to Coventry in the early Thirties to work as a cook at the Rootes factory. His memories of his father soon became hazy, yet with the onset of the Second World War, one of his pieces of oft-quoted wisdom was now at the forefront of John's mind. 'They only have wars to thin out the population, son,' his father had insisted. Sargent senior had, of course, been referring to a different war, in which millions of young men had been cut down in the prime of their lives. Now it seemed to John that civilians were on the front line as much as any soldier, especially civilians in cities like Coventry.

At the age of fourteen, John found employment as an apprentice at Humber, a car manufacturer that had recently been acquired by the Rootes brothers, who also won control of the Hillman line at the same time. Work was plentiful following the annual motor show, but workers faced redundancy in the inevitable six-month slow-down that followed. John was soon persuaded to become an apprentice at Modern Machine Tools, where work was steady. He went to night school to learn the fundamentals of engineering and was eventually working on 70-ton planing machines. But the day job was not his only interest. John had developed a fascination for first aid. When he moved to Coventry with his mother and brother in 1934, he joined the Boys' Brigade, where he soon made new friends and together they were spellbound by the First World War army sergeant who taught them rudimentary medical skills. Three years later, he joined the St John Ambulance Brigade to continue his first aid training. As the threat of war loomed, he and his colleagues practised in earnest. They learned how to tie bandages – then they tied them on each other in the dark so they were confident that they could work in blackouts. And after hours spent under tuition in the classroom, John and his colleagues could put a splint in place more quickly and efficiently than most hospital staff, something of vital importance for blast victims with shattered legs who had a far greater chance of recovery if their broken bones were kept from rubbing together and held steady.

The brigade members also learned how to drive ambulances by borrowing a vehicle from the station and driving it around fields nearby, taking turns at the controls. Some were better than others at driving and on many occasions John had been tossed around in the back as would-be ambulance drivers only narrowly avoided flipping the vehicle. Now their considerable efforts paid off. During emergencies, nurses and doctors were delighted to see an army of St John Ambulance-trained assistants to relieve the workload.

The early air raids in the autumn of 1940 added tales of breath-taking courage and empty despair to the annals of Coventry's history. On 17 October, 2nd Lieutenant Alexander Fraser Campbell, of 9 Bomb Disposal Company of the Royal Engineers, won a George Cross for his bravery in dealing with an unexploded bomb that had fallen on Coventry's Triumph Engineering Company. It kept 1,000 workers from their posts and caused an evacuation of local residents. Having worked for forty-eight hours, Lieutenant Campbell found it was impossible to remove the delayed action fuse. With the assistance of Lance Sergeant John Hinton, he took the difficult decision to remove the bomb from the site. On the torturous journey to the outskirts of the city, Campbell lay alongside it on the bed of the lorry, ready to shout a warning to the driver if he heard the ominous ticking sound that would indicate it had sprung to life. Fortunately, the journey was silent and Campbell carried out a controlled destruction of the bomb. Lance Sergeant Hinton was awarded the George Medal for his part in the drama.

By the next day, Campbell's luck had changed. He returned to a problematic 550-lb bomb that had fallen four days previously through the roof of a food wholesaler, E Laxon & Co, in Upper Well Street. Standard procedures had failed, but it was thought that the electrical charge that had been wired to detonate the bomb was by that time almost certainly dead. Working with another future George Cross winner, Sergeant Michael Gibson, and five other men, Campbell directed the loading of the bomb on to a lorry, which headed to Whitley Common at the edge of the city. It seemed a comparatively routine mission, but as the bomb was being taken off the lorry, it exploded without warning, killing all the men involved. Campbell, who was forty-two and from Ayrshire, left a widow, Agnes. In addition to thirty-four-year-old Sergeant Gibson, the other dead included Richard Gilchrest, twenty-three, from Manchester, Lancashire-born William Gibson, who was aged twenty-two, twenty-year-old Ronald Skelton from Cardiff and twenty-five-year-old Arthur Plumb – all of whom were from the same 9 Bomb Disposal Company – and the driver Lance Corporal Gordon Taylor, who was twenty-seven and came from Thornaby-on-Tees. He was a member of 17 Bomb Disposal Company.

Exemplary courage such as this was not the preserve of men, either. The story of Betty Popkiss who joined the St John Ambulance Brigade after leaving Barr Hill Girls Grammar School is a case in point. On the night of 19 October, Betty presented herself at the Air Raid Precautions post in Hen Lane in the district of Holbrooks as usual, it being the closest to her home. That night, like many others, the air raid began with a shower of incendiaries. She joined the willing team that rushed between blazes, armed with sand and earth to kill the flames. Despite a fear of heights, she shinned up a ladder to help one man put out an incendiary device that was smouldering in his roof, using a bucket and a stirrup pump.

When the larger bombs began to fall, she decided to make her way home. But before she got there, she met a little girl who lived on the same road. The distraught child ran up to Betty, crying, 'Mummy ... daddy ... please'. Betty dispatched her to the ARP post to raise the alarm and made for the girl's home. It was clear that the Anderson shelter used by the family had taken a direct hit and inside people were trapped and injured. Ominously, there were no cries for help, nor screams of terror. Instead, there were low moans that denoted serious injury. Instinctively, Betty set to work with her bare hands, but it was slow and arduous going. As luck would have it, a discarded shovel lay nearby and Betty set to work with renewed vigour. When she looked up, she saw a young boy on a bicycle watching her from the street. She urged him to go into the nearest house through a door blown open by the blast to collect blankets for the injured. When he proved reluctant, she began shouting her instructions more forcefully. 'Just go and do it,' she told him, jolting him into action.

Then others began arriving to help, their task lit only by the flares from exploding shells. Eventually, the occupants of the shelter were freed. There was a family of five and two other young girls. Without a second thought Betty put everything she had learned in the classroom into practice and administered first aid. Years later, she recalled how she had pulled off her highly prized, new, black coat to cover one of the injured without a second thought. Her courage that night also earned her a George Medal.

Between 18 August and the end of October, Coventry was attacked on seventeen occasions, including one by a solitary bomber who landed a single bomb on the paint shop of the Standard Motor Works at Canley. Lord Haw-Haw, also known as William Joyce, who delivered propaganda on the radio for Hitler, later reported that a pilot had been awarded the Iron Cross for bombing the factory and scornfully suggested that it was possible because the anti-aircraft gun crews were playing the 'early-closers' at football, a reference to the fact that all shops closed on a Thursday afternoon – the time of the raid – and that the shop workers had a football team.

All told, 198 tons of bombs were dropped, made up of 938 high explosives and 8,400 incendiaries. There were 176 dead, 229 badly injured and 451 minor injuries.

After one of these raids, a man found the back axle of a car in his back garden. 'Well,' he said. 'I always wanted a car but I didn't think I'd start with a back axle'.

Black humour was something of a hallmark of the Midlands, and Coventry folk possessed their fair share, which helped them to endure these straitened times. But for them, it was not entirely a case of 'make do and mend' or 'suffer in silence'.

Even before the Blitz, Coventry residents had a list of grievances that included the condition of air raid shelters, the scarcity of some food, concern about the Government's apparent inaction, the lack of anti-aircraft cover in the city and the inflexibility of factory hours. The daylight raid by the pilot mentioned by Lord Haw-Haw, caused waves of indignation among a population that felt increasingly vulnerable, given how disturbingly trigger-happy the pilot had been on his machine gun. But the government had concerns in addition to the escalating number of air raids in Britain. Ships were being lost at an increasing rate. During the week the Coventry Blitz took place, 76,182 tons of shipping was sunk, most of it British. Eight ships were holed by planes; five by U-boats; two small ships were victims of mines and four ships were the victims of a surface raider. Consequently, a diminishing amount of imports had reached Britain.

There were two capital ships, one cruiser, three anti-aircraft ships, fourteen armed merchant cruisers, thirty-eight destroyers and thirty-nine sloops and corvettes on escort duties, while German troops were massed in striking distance of Spain, Portugal and Bulgaria. At the same time Greece was seeking substantial cash from the British government to fend off German attentions.

Back in Coventry, people were learning to live under the threat of nightly attacks, but they could not possibly have foreseen the raid with which they were threatened, the most intense that had ever taken place.

On 8 November, the RAF bombed Munich, hailed in Germany as the birthplace of the Nazi party. The attack only narrowly missed Hitler himself and, the following day, an outraged Führer gave his skewed reasoning for the outrages to come. He insisted that the German Air Force had made no night raids on Poland, Norway, Holland, Belgium or France. 'Then, suddenly, Mr Churchill had bombs dropped on the German civil population. I waited in patience, thinking "The man is mad; for such action could only lead to Britain's destruction" ... Now I am resolved to fight it out to the last.

'It was the greatest military folly of all time that Mr Churchill committed in attempting to fight with the weakest of all his weapons.'

# Chapter Five

# 'Trying to hit a flying pheasant on a dark night with a rifle'

*Anonymous Anti-aircraft Commander*

By the autumn of 1940, it was clear that a new chapter in aerial warfare was about to begin. German strategists had in mind a hammer blow that would finally bring Britain to heel. It was now a case of laying its foundations. Pilots on both sides were trained in 'dead reckoning', a calculation of an aeroplane's whereabouts which was based on its last known position, and that still entailed getting a glimpse of the earth below, even at night, to achieve the necessary certainty for bombing missions.

Daylight raids carried out early in the war proved costly for both sides and lessons had been learned by the Luftwaffe as early as June after six aircraft were shot down over London in a low-flying attack. Consequently, the air chiefs decided to return to night-time bombing, which had been favoured by airships in the First World War. But in darkness, there were navigational difficulties that were often exacerbated by poor weather – even when the targets were in sprawling cities. In the Great War, when the military and the moral imperative was to bomb industry rather than people, not a single factory had been hit and since then ground-based defences had improved. Now, it was widely accepted that a pilot's best hope of returning to base was by bombing from on high and 'blind' to avoid barrage balloons and anti-aircraft fire. For the Germans, it would not prove to be such a problem.

There were two developments already being refined at the start of the war which helped the Luftwaffe to find its targets even at great altitude. The German Air Force began using the radio beam bombing system *Knickebein*, or 'Crooked Leg', rooted in pioneering work carried out in Germany during the Thirties. It involved projecting two invisible signals so that they intersected over a pre-determined target. A pilot travelled along one beam, listening carefully for the steady tone that told him he was on the right path. The sound of dots or dashes in place of the tone indicated that he had strayed off course. When the first beam intersected with a second, the tone changed and the pilot knew it was time to dispatch the ordnance. Any number of aeroplanes could use the beams once they were established. The system was accurate to within about one mile, with the beam coming from a beacon some 180 miles distant. The obvious drawback was that, given the right technology, it could be jammed.

A second target-seeking method was also introduced, involving a fan of fine beams and cross beams called the X-system. With this innovation, there were several intersections that gave pilots a series of warnings about how far they were away from their target during a long, straight approach. Once again, pilots would know by a change in the tenor of the beams whether they were adrift, with the sound issued from the new *X-Gerät* equipment installed in their aircraft. Transmitters of the beams could be fixed at a particular site – after the fall of France, the Channel coast was extensively used – or transported to suitable areas on the back of a lorry. Its accuracy was even better than that previously achieved with *Knickebein*. The promise of precision bombing that would not unduly endanger civilians at last seemed a reality and pilots, along with wireless operators and observers, found it simple to use. Externally, aeroplanes with *X-Gerät* could be distinguished by two additional radio masts on the rear fuselage.

Despite the huge potential of *X-Gerät* – or *X-Verfahren* as it was also known in Germany – it was not initally deployed as widely and as quickly as it could have been.

Internal squabbles hampered its being fitted in Luftwaffe aeroplanes prior to the war and, as a consequence, the system was still being trialled in the winter of 1939–40. After one aeroplane crashed in the North Sea, the *X-Gerät* was even removed from some aircraft for fear of the secret falling into British hands. But by the summer of 1940, the Luftwaffe was using both systems during attacks across Britain. Together, these subtly different technologies offered plenty for the British to puzzle and pore over.

The Royal Air Force's Wireless Intelligence Service soon discovered the *Knickebein* beams – appropriately codenamed 'Headaches' by the British. In March 1940, a Heinkel He 111 was shot down, and in the wreckage there was a paper containing some tantalising clues, including the name and a frequency. The following month, another aeroplane was brought down – strangely with the same identifying code as the first, implying it was the replacement – with a diary note from the pilot stating 'In the afternoon, studied about Knickebein'.

As an antidote, 'Aspirin' transmitters were developed, which were responsible for beam interference. German navigation signals were also intercepted and re-broadcast in a technique known as 'meaconing' that was used from July 1940.

At first, British scientists thought that no beams had the capacity to spread across the English landscape from a transmitter sited on foreign soil. So had the necessary beacons been secretly installed in the British countryside? A search of an area defined by coordinates gleaned from German messages came up with nothing. Intelligence officers also considered the possibility that *Knickebein* was nothing more than an elaborate German hoax. Then, on 14 June, a German prisoner, who had been shot down over Norway, confirmed under interrogation that *Knickebein* was real enough and had the capability of dropping bombs accurately and automatically. The system had been used in the battle for Warsaw, he said, and had been improved since then. He confirmed that beams were transmitted from towers and his sketch of them tallied with a number of buildings spotted on reconnaissance photographs that had been perplexing intelligence officers for some time. Now scientists and top brass had a good grasp of the theory related behind *Knickebein*, it was time to seek proof positive.

On 21 June, an aeroplane was sent up manned by two people with experience of radio frequency recognition but armed with only sketchy details about the project and nothing of what was known so far. When they landed, the pair confirmed that a narrow beam was passing one mile south of Spalding, concurring with German information, with dots to the south and dashes to the north. A second beam with similar characteristics, but this time with dots to the north and dashes to the south, passed somewhere near Beeston.

A report sent to Winston Churchill on 28 June, written by Dr Reginald Jones who was on the front line in the battle of the beams, said how 'in the course of ten days the matter has developed from a conjecture to a certainty ... some technical points remain to be cleared up but their elucidation is only a matter of time.'

By September, the threat from *Knickebein* was largely diminished by British counter-electronic measures, about which German pilots were only dimly aware. According to Winston Churchill, 'The German pilots followed the beam as the German people followed the Führer. They had nothing else to follow.' Simplistically, he claimed that the British countermeasures to the *Knickebein* beams sent pilots off course to harmlessly bomb open fields. To illustrate his point, he explained how the wife and two young children of a Whitehall colleague sent to the country to escape air raids had seen a series of a hundred heavy bombs being dropped close by – some ten miles from the nearest town.

Yet, Churchill was perhaps too quick to discredit the German Air Force, which, with more beam technology available to it, may have had a different agenda in mind.

There is every reason to believe that at least some of the apparently unsuccessful raids by the Luftwaffe were carried out for training purposes by pilots getting a feel for *X-Gerät*. A happy bi-product for the German war effort was the chaos they caused in doing so. Even a handful of German aeroplanes roaming around the night skies was sufficient for the sirens to be sounded in cities up and down Britain. For example, on 31 August, Coventry was paralysed by an air-raid warning for five hours; Liverpool for six; Manchester for four and Portsmouth for five, while enemy action was barely noticeable. Each time the siren sounded – alternatively dubbed 'old moaner', 'moaning minnie' and 'wailing winnie' – families headed for their air raid shelters for a night of disrupted sleep. Above ground, Civil Defence personnel manned designated posts, straining their eyes and ears for evidence of anything incoming. Often, it was a false alarm and sometimes the siren – and subsequently the All Clear – sounded several times a night. Nuisance raids like these undoubtedly nibbled away at morale and dented industrial output, so the British decided to sound the siren less often. There was even a school of thought voiced in government that the siren should not be sounded at all.

All this time the *X-Gerät* was proving a formidable obstacle for British scientists. No one knew if it was the same or different from the *Knickebein*. A new series of transmissions detected in September implied that they were not alike. Fortunately, the scientists – unsung heroes of the fight against Nazism – began to unravel the beam mystery, albeit from a standing start. Information from Bletchley Park, where Germany's encoded messages were being unscrambled, helped to fill in some pieces of the jigsaw. The British learned that, while *Knickebein* had been standard in German aircraft, *X-Gerät* was fitted in only a few. The Heinkel He 111s flown by Kampfgruppe 100, based in Vannes, in Brittany, were the selected aircraft, something of an élite group that was distinguished by its Viking long boat emblem. It was these aircraft that were involved in an increasing number of incendiary attacks across Britain in October. Ultimately, they became trailblazers, literally and metaphorically. In full-blown raids, these Heinkels formed the first wave in an attack and the incendiaries they dropped lit the way for subsequent squadrons. For now, they operated alone, perfecting the art of night attack.

Intelligence officers soon knew enough to establish a series of 'Bromide' transmitters, which attempted to scramble the *X-Gerät* navigation signals. However, evidence shows that, initially at least, German pilots could easily spot the discrepancy between their own signals and the intruder variety. Then, the British had an amazing breakthrough. On 6 November 1940, a Heinkel He 111 fitted with *X-Gerät* equipment crash landed in West Bay, near Bridport, Dorset. Mystified by its *X-Gerät* readings, the lost pilot and crew imagined themselves to be in Spain. Only the sight of khaki-clad Tommies marching towards them confirmed that the transmitter meddling by the British had on this occasion been successful, in conjunction with a catastrophic compass failure. Soldiers guarded the wreck, which the RAF analysts badly wanted to examine. However, it was the Royal Navy that insisted on salvaging the crashed plane, saturating it in seawater as they towed it out to sea. Accordingly, valuable information about the *X-Gerät*, which was used so effectively to bomb Coventry twelve days later, did not become clear to investigators until the beginning of December.

The four German airmen who survived the crash were taken prisoner and subjected to intensive interrogation at a base near Barnet in Hertfordshire, known as Cockfosters Camp, the destination for all captured Luftwaffe men. (With no land-based battles at the time, there were no prisoners from the German Army.) Prisoners provided valuable intelligence, sometimes inadvertently. Apart from the grilling they experienced at the hands of RAF officers, their conversations were bugged in one of a dozen rooms that had been wired for sound and the recordings were used to get a better picture of German plans.

Surveillance techniques were still in their early days, but one refinement introduced in December 1940 was to plant a German or Austrian refugee as a roommate of captured Luftwaffe fliers. Later, stool pigeons included pilots and crew who had grown sick of the conflict. For now, investigators could only sit and listen, and eavesdropping on German prisoners furnished the British with various pieces of information about *X-Gerät*, although most pilots were much more conversant with *Knickebein*.

Often, they spoke highly of the technology that they had at their fingertips, believing it ruled out human error. The *X-Gerät* equipment did indeed include an automatic bombing clock that was activated by the beams. When the hands of the clock overlapped, the incendiaries were released. But with morale dipping in the absence of the swift victory that the Luftwaffe had expected, some airmen were sceptical about the efficacy of both systems. If they were so fail-safe, one pilot observed dryly, 'then I can't understand why London still exists'.

Prisoner discussions also elaborated on flak accuracy, the effectiveness of the balloon barrage and the damage being inflicted on Germany by RAF raids. A dedicated interrogator called Samuel Felkin, an RAF officer who was responsible for questioning all German Air Force prisoners, listened in to all talk about *X-Gerät* and how it worked. Then he heard some information that was altogether less technical.

On 11 November, a POW in conversation with a room-mate revealed that a colossal raid had been planned. The timescale he gave was between 15 and 20 November, which would coincide with a full moon. Coventry and Birmingham were the targets, he confided.

An official report from the time says that information 'from another source' named the operation Moonlight Sonata. The other source was almost certainly the code breakers at Bletchley Park, whose work was still a closely guarded secret. The following day, more intelligence was made available which pointed to the involvement of the élite

KG-100 Pathfinders as well as Luftwaffe Air Fleets 2 and 3 and that Göring himself was controlling the operation. And this was the background to a scandal that enveloped Churchill forty years after the raid on Coventry.

When the veil of secrecy that surrounded the work done at Bletchley Park was finally lifted in the early Seventies, two books sensationally blamed Churchill for sacrificing Coventry rather than reveal that he knew the intended target of a big raid before it took place. If he had done so, the books claimed, he would have betrayed the existence of the top-secret code breakers. The accusation was criticised by historians, who pointed out that Churchill altered his plans in order to watch the raid unfold, believing the target was London. Of course, no one knows what Churchill knew at the time, but what he was told is known.

A report from the Air Ministry, dated 12 November, listed the likely targets as central London, Harwich/Ipswich, Greater London and the triangle bounded by Farnborough Aerodrome, Reading and Maidenhead or Kent. And it was this information that was sent to the Prime Minister on 14 November in a memo that stated that the attack was not likely to take place before 15 November. It also elaborated on snippets of information gleaned from a POW shot down on 9 November: '[The prisoner] states that Göring is convinced that the people in London are on the point of revolution and that Buckingham Palace has been stormed. He has therefore arranged a great raid to take place on Coventry and Birmingham with the object of destroying workers' dwellings in order to undermine the morale of the working classes.'

For reasons it does not explain, the memo still favoured London as the likely target in spite of the testimony of the captured airman. Perhaps he was not trusted because his information about Buckingham Palace was so wide of the mark. 'If further information indicates Coventry, Birmingham or elsewhere we hope to get out instructions in time,' the note to Churchill concluded.

Winston Churchill had been planning to go to the Prime Minister's country residence, Chequers, that night. But after he read the contents of the latest, top-secret report that he had received during the car journey, he ordered his chauffeur to turn round and he spent the night on the Air Ministry roof, apparently ready to survey the raid. The vast majority of historians believe it was where he genuinely believed the bombs would fall. A few people still think it was part of an elaborate charade.

What could Churchill have done if he had had a warning about the Coventry raid? There was certainly no precedent for evacuating a city perceived to be under threat from aerial bombers and it has never happened since. Fighter aeroplanes were already on alert as they inevitably were when Britain was subject to nightly attacks. If Churchill wanted to keep the extent of the code breaking a secret, that would be understandable. But the evidence that flagged up the raid seems to have come from a prisoner, whose information was merely backed up by Bletchley Park. While there was an obvious desire to shield the work carried out at Bletchley Park from public gaze, there was little virtue in protecting the reputation of Luftwaffe personnel locked up at Cockfosters Camp and it could have been made known that this was the source of any Blitz warning. In any event, air staff aimed to counter Operation Moonlight Sonata with a plan of their own, called Operation Cold Water.

In a report written on 13 November, the expectation was for three attacks to be carried out on successive nights.

Principally, the RAF counter-strategy consisted of a six-point plan that was aimed at restricting the effects of any one of them:

1 There was to be a close watch on German radio activity, while unleashing maximum radio interference upon enemy navigational beams and beacons.

2 Security patrols by bomber aircraft over German aerodromes occupied by Air Fleets 2 and 3 were to be instigated.

3 A large attack against the aerodrome at Vannes in Brittany was planned, the home of KG-100, described at the Air Ministry as 'specialist beam flyers'.

4 There were to be bombing raids on the *Knickebein* and VHF beams, as *X-Gerät* was then termed, at Cherbourg by aircraft flying up the beams to locate the diminutive target and dropping sticks of bombs.

5 A heavy bombing attack on a selected city in Germany was outlined.

6 Concentrated fire against the Luftwaffe by night fighters and anti-aircraft artillery was also promised.

One report from the Air Ministry written in response to the plans for Operation Cold Water offered slightly different ideas. It argued that there should be security patrols over 30 Luftwaffe aerodromes rather than just a select few: 'The [British] bomber should not arrive and throw its bombs on the aerodrome and come home, but should be armed with the largest number of small bombs possible and stay in the vicinity of the enemy aerodome as long as possible, throwing a bomb when it is apparent that aircraft are taking off – or at irregular intervals.'

The actions of the heavy bomber force needed careful consideration, it said, revealing early indications of the 'knock for knock' idea that was evolving there:

> To pour cold water on the Moonlight Sonata we should remember that if the maximum scale of night attack is concentrated on a place like London or Birmingham no matter what we do serious superficial damage will be done and high casualties caused – quite apart from any key point that may be hit.
>
> In consequence we should remember that the best way of turning cold water on an operation of this kind from the point of John Citizen is to hit back at a similarly important area in Germany as hard as we can.

When increased beam activity and enemy reconnaissance communications were reported at 1.00 p.m. on the day of the raid, Operation Cold Water was duly activated. Some elements of it were undeniably successful. Within two hours, it became clear that all the beams intersected over Coventry and all RAF Commands were subsequently informed. Only at this point could an evacuation procedure have swung into action. (It is worth remembering that when London was being bombed night after night and there was absolute certainty it would be a target, no official framework existed for the evacuation of its residents.)

Coventry was by no means a defenceless city. It had the same tools in its armoury as other industrial centres thought to be key Luftwaffe targets. Night fighters were only part of this three-pronged strategy – but their companion elements were equally flawed. Searchlights and anti-aircraft artillery were the ground-based defences against aerial attack but, operating in concert with fighters, the trio managed to bring down just 117 German machines from British skies between June and October.

Searchlights were acknowledged as the only way of improving night vision for the anti-aircraft gunners, but their effectiveness was curbed by cloud cover in a country where rain was commonplace even in summer. Conversely, on bright, moonlit nights the searchlight beams were hardly visible at all. Then there was the question of range. The upper limit of the searchlight was 12,000ft so any aircraft flying above that could do so without being spotted. In reality, the help they offered anti-aircraft gunners was negligible.

The work of the anti-air craft gunner was 'like trying to hit a flying pheasant on a dark night with a rifle', according to one commander, although the sound of anti-aircraft guns was acknowledged as a morale booster for nearby civilians. Still, searchlight operators also hoped to help night fighters by silhouetting the enemy despite the blackened undercarriages of Luftwaffe bombers. Yet the hoped for cooperation amounted to little more than wishful thinking.

As early as 1938, it was realised that a target had to be illuminated for eight minutes to enable a fighter to close and engage fire. Few enemy aircraft were obliging enough to stay in the path of lights for that long. None of the difficulties outlined above should denigrate the courage that was shown by searchlight operators who often found themselves in the firing line. Enemy fighters might swoop down from bomber escort duty in a bid to extinguish the beam by firepower. A bomber might even make it a specific target.

There is no doubt that the authorities were aware of the limitations of 1930s air defences. In 1934, the Air Ministry established a committee for the Scientific Survey of Air Defence in response to concerns. It expressed lofty ambitions, including aerial minefields, infra-red detection, the installation of searchlights in planes and even the development of a death ray. Fortunately, any Government spare cash was devoted to the development of a truly effective weapon. By the time the war started, radar – albeit rudimentary in its scope – could detect enemy aircraft at a distance if the flight path was above the height of 2,000ft. This allowed a chain of coastal radar stations to warn fighter bases when and from where enemy formations were approaching British airspace. That alone saved Coastal Command a small fortune by eliminating the need for costly patrols.

But there were no radar stations inland to take up the baton. After the Luftwaffe crossed the coastline, it was the job of the Observer Corps to track their path, 'a transition from the middle of the twentieth century to the early stone age', according to Winston Churchill when he was part of the air defence committee. Highly trained though these men of the Corps were in the identification of aircraft, they needed clear daylight to be certain of their conclusions. In cloudy weather and at night, enemy aircraft had to be located by sound alone. To say it was an inexact science at the time would be an understatement. In short, these men listened for aircraft, only sometimes with the help of echo-location equipment. But even with the benefit of basic equipment, there was no way they could discern the height of the aircraft and two machines were frequently mistaken for one, because of their increasing speed capabilities.

There was an improvement with the arrival of radar and at least one site in Coventry was furnished with it before the Blitz. There were forty high-angle guns defending the city and these are said to have remained in action throughout the bombardment on 14 November. Although the gun operations room was bombed, it soon returned to action.

The number of light anti-aircraft at the city's disposal had been increased on 12 November by twelve Bofors guns provided by Home Forces.

Like other cities, Coventry had barrage balloons designed to deter low-flying aircraft.

As it happened, the Coventry barrage of fifty-six balloons was reinforced on 14 November by the delivery of a further sixteen, eight of which were deployed that night. Although there were many more barrage balloons in neighbouring Birmingham, both Portsmouth and Southampton had a similar number. No enemy aircraft came below the level of the balloons, but as it turned out, they did not need to try.

# Chapter Six

# 'We didn't bother if we lived or died, so you can just imagine how we felt.'

*Mary Latham*

A first indication that enemy planes were heading for Coventry was probably received by the people of Lyme Bay, who may have heard a distant engine throb as they retreated from the cold night air into their dimly lit homes.

This was the initial wave of Heinkel He 111s loaded with more than 2,200lb of incendiaries. They made landfall at 6.17 p.m. under the scrutiny of coastal radar stations and headed for the Midlands city via Bristol.

Every time the siren had sounded in Coventry – and sometimes before the banshee wail began – there was a chorus of dog barks around the city. This time the cacophony of yips and yaps was drowned out because, as soon as the siren sounded at 7.10 p.m., the first bombs began to fall. Those below could not have known whether it would be a full-blown raid or a short-lived scare, as Birmingham or another nearby city took a pounding. Some had already gathered together bare necessities and headed for the rural outskirts.

It became routine at the sound of the siren, or even before, for a number of people to catch buses or cadge lifts to Leamington, Rugby, Kenilworth or Warwick since all of those towns were deemed less dangerous than Coventry. Advertisements offering accommodation for reasonable rates had started to appear some time before. The less wealthy left on foot, carrying the items they needed for the night in prams or wheelbarrows. With the number of kindly home owners who would offer their spare beds to Coventry folk by now diminishing, the only option for an unfortunate few was to sleep in barns or under hedges. Tile Hill Woods was a favourite destination. Those who left regularly were known as 'trekkers' and were thought to amount to between a quarter and a half of the city's population.

Wardens marked houses known to be empty with the letters SO in chalk, standing for 'sleeps out'. That way no time would be wasted looking for people who were not there in the event of a direct hit. However, there was some resentment directed towards trekkers by people who believed everyone was obliged to stay in case fires in empty properties went unnoticed and endangered other homes nearby.

Christina and Len Stephenson, by now already engaged, were among the trekkers that night, leaving their respective family homes to cycle to Fillongley village hall, eight miles to the north of Coventry. All night, they sat side by side, bolt upright on the hall's wooden benches, alongside dozens of others who had sought sanctuary there, watching Coventry's conflagration gather momentum.

The choice of possessions that people took from their homes was diverse: library books, documents, knitting, wedding presents with sentimental value or maybe the meat safe that stored weekly rations from the butcher's shop in the absence of refrigerators. On the night of the raid, one couple tore down a fitted wardrobe in their newly occupied home which had been completed only the previous day, saying 'that was wood, good wood, and wood was getting scarce'. Some people went to their Anderson shelters, some to the numerous public shelters. Others chose to stay inside their local pubs. There were more pubs on street corners then and they had cellars which offered potentially better protection than surface shelters.

At the time the Heinkels were crossing the southern coast, Len Dacombe was cycling to work to join the nightshift at Coventry Climax. He looked skywards to see the light of a full moon radiating across frosty Coventry roads as the sirens began echoing through the streets. He had already popped in to see his girlfriend Cecilia in Earlsdon. Since the pair first met at St Margaret's Hall in Ball Hill, Coventry in 1934, they had been a devoted couple. On that day, Len had been to watch Coventry's football team, which at that time was in the Third Division South and playing in black and red. He had been accompanied by a friend who persuaded him to go on to a dancing class. Within moments, Cecilia was his partner and they had stayed together ever since.

'If the Germans come tonight at least we will get a good view of them,' he commented wryly when he left her that evening.

As he drew up to the junction with Holyhead Road, he heard a sinister droning. The distinctive turn of the engine told him this was a wave of German aircraft, rather than British. The streets were deserted, and Len scolded himself for obeying the traffic laws when there was no one about. With sharp shadows from the moonlight and the whining from above, the city he had known for years suddenly seemed an eerie and hostile place. By the time he arrived at Coventry Climax in Widdrington Road at just after 7.00 p.m., there had already been a shower of incendiary bombs. Wooden bins that contained the parts made by the factory flared like kindling. A fellow worker put out one of the blazes with an overcoat. The nightshift workers – scheduled to work until

7.00 a.m. – gathered for a meeting. They decided the only sensible option was to find shelter. However, Len – a special constable in his spare time – immediately offered to help with fire watching at the factory. He was also the night-shift charge hand responsible for the machinery.

When Len had first arrived in Coventry in 1931 to find work as an apprentice, he had had several jobs, lasting a matter of months or a year. British industry was still stuttering after the depression of the late Twenties. Only when he joined Coventry Climax, initially at its Friars Road factory, did the threat of prolonged unemployment finally end.

The factory had once made car engines, but worked its way out of recession by producing water pumps for fire fighters. With the advent of the Second World War, Coventry Climax became a key manufacturer, Len was determined to protect the factory whose management had shown sufficient faith in him to promote him earlier that year, when he moved to the firm's site in Widdrington Road. So he joined the regular factory fire watchers in a small brick shelter in the middle of the machine shop to watch and wait.

As always, the sound of the siren brought a quiver of apprehension for sixteen-year-old Alan Hartley. It had become a familiar sound during his teenage years. Earlier generations had marked their adolescent years with the lively rhythm of jazz or its younger cousin, swing. But for Alan and thousands of others, it was a tuneless moan that defined most of his evenings. He had been poised to take his school certificate in 1939, but the declaration of war put an end to any academic ambitions and, instead of moving from the grammar school into further education, he became an apprentice at Alfred Herbert Limited which made machine tools.

Alan lived in Grayswood Avenue with his father Harold, his mother Alice and his younger sister Joyce. They were neighbours of Mary Bloomfield whose diary has been referred to earlier. His older brother Leslie had already joined the Royal Engineers and was among those who escaped from Dunkirk.

Harold Hartley had been a shipwright in Barrow-in-Furness, but moved to Coventry along with others when orders for new ships dried up, and became a carpenter working on the huge estates that were being built. Although he had been compelled to leave school, Alan remained in the Air Training Corps and was also a messenger with the Air Raid Precautions Service, which had been created in 1937 as the spectre of war loomed. Its aim was to get local people to patrol areas to enforce the blackout, guide people to shelters, rescueg those who had been bombed and fight small fires. Alan was among the youngest in the ARP outfit. Sixteen was deemed to be the minimum age to join and even then parental consent was required.

It was to ARP Post 607 that Alan headed at the sound of the siren, which was located at the top of his road. He had no uniform save his black, steel helmet, marked with a white 'M' that denoted he was a messenger. Within moments, lights in the sky caught his eye. One flare appeared over Coundon, then another over Radford, then Allesley and Earlsdon. Before his astonished gaze, the entire city became ringed with bright lights each descending slowly, its progress measured by a small parachute. This was, he knew, a navigational aid for German bombers who were surely not far away.

At first, the sound was muffled, then it became louder. It was the unmistakeable crump of bombs, dropping ever closer. Running as hard as he could, Alan arrived at the post to find it at action stations. He and the other members of the ARP were dispatched with wardens to help defend their community against the aerial raiders.

Incendiaries, used by all protagonists in the conflict, were perhaps the most effective of all the weapons of the Second World War. One estimate suggested that they were responsible for three-quarters of all damage to buildings worldwide. In 1940, the Luftwaffe was typically arming its planes with 2-lb incendiaries, measuring about 14in long. They were packed with highly flammable thermite that ignited on impact. A green tail fin helped to direct the bomb in its downward descent and it was built to punch a hole in a tiled roof before bursting into white-hot flames.

For the first time in the Coventry raid, some of the incendiaries contained a seven-minute delay before erupting into a small fireball, with the aim of spraying its molten casing or magnesium charge over approaching firefighters. Incendiaries were often used in the opening stages of a raid, but that night they were dropped throughout.

Bombers were fitted with racks, known as breadbaskets, to hold the incendiaries securely during a flight. The breadbaskets came in various sizes, the largest holding somewhere in the order of 700 devices. At the signal of the Luftwaffe's *X-Gerät* they were automatically released from the bomb hatches of this first wave of Heinkels onto the target below in the knowledge that small fires would quickly link up to create a firestorm. Oil bombs, which were also used in the Coventry raid, are usually classed as incendiaries although these weigh in at 550lbs.

ARP wardens were used to dealing with the smaller German incendiary devices and, by November 1940, householders had also been shown how to douse them by

101

extinguishing the flames as quickly as possible using sand or water that were kept at the ready in buckets. Most people had access to a stirrup pump, a manually operated device that sucked water from a bucket through a hose, the nozzle of which could be set as a jet or spray. A public information film about stirrup pumps which was shown at cinemas advised making sixty-five pushes on the pump handle to maintain a jet of water while only thirty-five were needed for a spray. As the length of hose could be unreeled and taken to a blaze some distance from the pump, it was a two-person job. Drenching incendiaries required quick work, but before this raid, it had not been an unduly hazardous task.

Together with a warden, Alan and several other messengers arrived at the fence ringing the neighbouring rifle fields to find a mass of small fires. Quickly, they shinned over the 4-ft wooden fence, gripping shovels, but realised that they did not have ready access to the sand or water that was needed to put out the flames.

Looking around by his feet, Alan saw that cows had recently grazed the field and had left generous quantities of their familiar calling card. In a flash, he heaved some cow dung on to a nearby incendiary and watched with satisfaction as the heat of it dried it out the dung until it became like a hardened shell. With no oxygen to feed the fire, the flames died away. He shouted to the others nearby to tell them what he had done, and working hard and fast, they used nature's finest fire extinguisher until the field was once again in darkness.

Courage in the face of the incendiary threat was not the preserve of the young or the uniformed. As the raid escalated, one seventy-year-old Coventry woman was spotted by a neighbour scooping up incendiaries with a dustpan and brush and putting them in a galvanised dustbin. Thanks to the new style explosive incendiary, though, it was not always as straightforward as this. William Wilson, who later became an MP for Coventry, was using a shovel to throw sand on an incendiary when it erupted in his face. The shovel was ripped from his grip by its force. Dazed and partially blinded, he spent the rest of the evening in a public shelter before reporting to the Gulson Road first-aid centre for treatment. This kind of incendiary 'put me off fireworks for a long time', one survivor remarked dryly.

Like everywhere else, the hospital and its grounds were being showered by incendiaries. Dr Harry Winter, who stood on a flat roof of the building to witness the grounds glowing with fires, was put in mind of a different public celebration as the numerous small-scale blazes were 'like lights twinkling on a mammoth Christmas tree': 'Down below in the light of other fires which were already lighting up the sky over the city I could see the men of the hospital staff running from bomb to bomb, dousing them in buckets of sand. I heard later that some of the male patients spent most of the night in the grounds putting out incendiaries.'

At the sound of the siren, families began a series of well-worn routines. Beryl Ann Leadley's mother picked up a loaf of bread, the butter dish and a knife and took them down the air-raid shelter along with her children in case her family got hungry. As always, the family's Anderson shelter in Moseley Avenue, in Coundon, was soggy underfoot. Beryl sat upright on the back of the bench with her feet on its seat to keep them dry. They passed the time by counting the bombs as they came down. After counting four, they felt the immediate danger had passed. Then, with unremitting regularity, the next batch could be heard: 'The nearest bomb we had was in the garden next door. The old couple who lived there were in their shelter, buried up to their armpits in soil.'

At 6.00 p.m., nineteen-year-old Mary Latham had returned to her home in Hampton Road, in Foleshill, from her job at Brico, which made piston rings. She had been working there since her fourteenth birthday, starting on a wage of 11 shillings a week. At first, her job was polishing piston rings with emery paper, rubbing off the metal burrs until her hands bled. She was now an inspector earning £4 a week, money that she gave directly to her widowed mother. In return, she was given pocket money in an arrangement that continued until she was twenty-five. Her father Robert had been a miner in Wales before moving to the pit near Coventry. Then he worked at Armstrong Siddeley before his death, when Mary was aged seven. After he died, her mother received a pension of 10 shillings a week at a time when the rent amounted to 8s 8d. The family survived only because her mother kept two allotments. Her eldest brother Leslie – sacked from Daimler after denting Queen Mary's car during an indoor game of football – was in the RAF and her younger brother Harry had joined the Royal Navy. Her sisters lived locally, except for one who had been evacuated to Wales. Although she wanted to join one of the services, Mary felt that she could not leave her mother.

That night, Mary got changed, expecting to spend the night in the family's Anderson shelter, and put in her curlers. But her mother decided they should find more substantial protection, sensing that the raid was going to be bigger than usual. Together with her sisters Edith and Susan, they went to an air-raid shelter attached to a flourmill in Swanswell, where Mary's brother-in-law worked. They were almost there when the siren first sounded and they only narrowly missed being caught in the first wave of incendiaries. Soon after the raid, Mary wrote an eight-page letter to her sister Marge in Wales, describing what had happened to the family that night when the bombs crashed down 'like a thunderstorm':

> We didn't bother if we lived or died, so you can just imagine how we felt.
>
> For the first start-off, Jimmy Walsh out of the mill came down the cellar with all his face burnt.
>
> This was caused by one of those exploding incendiary bombs.
>
> Then in came Tommy Nutt [another mill worker], the same had happened to him.
>
> They were both laying there in a state.
>
> They had to, as we could not get the ambulance, they were all out on duty.
>
> We all started to make our beds thinking we should go to sleep.

In fact, Mary's sister Edith slept throughout it all, but her mother Florence shook with fear. 'Mam was ever so bad,' wrote Mary. 'I felt ever so sorry for her and we couldn't help her in any way. We had no whisky, no brandy or nothing. We all sat there, parched.'

Often, people dashed in and out of shelters, either to help fight fires or to use the shelter as a pit-stop on a journey through the city. Betty Daniel spent the night in the family's Anderson shelter, where there were comings and goings all the time. Men from the family were outside, busily putting incendiary bombs out until the approaching whistle of a bomb brought them into the shelter at speed.

With the initial chaos caused by the pathfinder Heinkels, no one was particularly aware as they hunkered down that a phalanx of bombers had arrived over Coventry from the Lincolnshire coast, quickly followed by a third wave from French airfields from the south. Incendiaries now partially gave way to high explosives. In their armoury, the Luftwaffe bombers had the SC1000 bomb – nicknamed the Hermann. Measuring 8ft long and filled with Amatol and TNT, these bombs were so hefty that a Heinkel could carry only two at a time. The Hermann was designed to blow out the walls of buildings and was thought to be particularly suited to bringing down factories.

Guided to the city by the fires already in progress, each bomber group was aiming for a particular target. One had the Standard Motor Car Company and Coventry Radiator and Press Work Co Ltd in its sights, while a second was detailed to attack Alvis Aero Engine Works. A third headed for the gas holders in Hill Street as well as Cornercraft Ltd, and a further group of aircraft sought to destroy the British Piston Ring Company and the Daimler Works.

As the combined might of the Luftwaffe let loose its bombs, John Sargent dashed to the shelter in Henry Street, which had taken a direct hit early on. The brick walls of this recently built surface shelter had been blown out and the concrete roof intended to protect those inside had fallen in. The design of public shelters was notoriously poor and many had been put up at speed as war approached. Desperately, John's eyes raked over the rubble, searching out an entry point. When he saw a small opening, he ripped off his tin hat and crawled in.

For a moment, the low cries of those inside rose above the sound of whistling bombs. Nobody was dead – but it was not possible to drag anyone to safety. Although it had fractured into pieces, the concrete debris was too hefty to move and chunks of the roof were pinning people to the floor. Little could be done for the thirty people trapped inside without heavy lifting gear and while the raid continued, it was impossible to bring machinery like that into action. John slithered out the way he had come and ran to the hospital, returning moments later with a nurse and doctor who crawled inside and administered morphine, a powerful painkiller. There was no time to dwell on the eventual fate of the people in the shelter because casualties had begun to flood in at the hospital.

Most patients had already been brought down from the upper wards to the lower corridors for their own safety. However, two sets of patients could not be moved without exacerbating their condition. Accordingly, women with gynaecological problems were left in beds on the top floor, along with fracture patients who had been rendered immobile, as their arms or legs were suspended from metal arms. When the nurses' quarters nearby were bombed, these patients ended up covered in glass and throughout the raid they had an extraordinarily fine view of the waves of planes that were setting the city alight.

There was one other patient left on the top floor until all those who could be moved were safe. It was a injured German airman who had been captured after one of the October raids. Hospital staff remembered how, when he was finally retrieved, he moaned in fear in a way that none of the British patients had.

At 8.30 p.m., the men's and women's medical wards and the eye ward were evacuated. Nurses dashed along, pushing wheeled beds, while doctors, orderlies and sometimes other male patients gave the bed-bound piggy-backs to take them out of harm's way. Moments later, the men's medical ward was flattened by a bomb.

* * *

Like many, one schoolgirl spent the first part of the raid sheltering in the cupboard under the stairs. As she tried to concentrate on her maths homework of fractions, the windows of the house in Gregory Avenue shattered and the walls shook with each nearby bomb blast. During a lull in the raid, she and her family left the house for a neighbour's shelter. As she made her way there, she noticed how the moon reflected brightly on the carpet of broken glass that crunched beneath her feet.

Other families made similar decisions to flee their homes when it became apparent that the raid was heavier and more prolonged than any previously experienced. Alan Leadley and his father, who had moved to Coventry in July 1940 after failing to secure a steady job in their native Hull, were among them. The east-coast town had been bombed regularly before they left, but it was nothing in comparison to the scale of the assault that Coventry was currently experiencing. Alan's mother and brother were trekkers, while he and his father used to shelter under the table when the bombs started dropping. When the intensity of the attack became apparent, his father decided to take him to the shelter next door that belonged to a paper shop.

His father jumped into the Anderson shelter first, straight into about two feet of water. Then he pulled Alan inside and placed the youngster on a top bunk where his feet would not get wet. The accommodating newsagent suddenly realised that he did not have his cash tin. He dashed out to retrieve it, bringing back with him a bottle of whisky and 200 Senior Service cigarettes. Armed with a shovel, the newsagent and Alan's father, who brandished a fork, made periodic forays into the night to smother incendiaries. Most of the whisky and the cigarettes were gone by the morning.

Some families chose to stay in their houses for as long as possible. Thomas Cunningham-Boothe was dispatched to the family's shelter with blankets, while his mother remained in their home to finish ironing along with his youngest sister. Until that night, war had been a cause of great excitement for Thomas, as he collected bits of shrapnel and felt himself being lifted off the ground by the force of the nearby naval anti-aircraft gun when it fired. But it was at this point that the brutal reality of aerial warfare became starkly apparent. When she realised the ferocity of the raid, Thomas's mother called to her daughter to go into the cupboard under the stairs and she was about to stretch a protective arm around the teenager when the house in Lythalls Lane, Holbrooks, was shattered by a bomb.

Thomas's mother was hurled outside and covered in rubble. Already encumbered by an artificial leg, she had to loosen the harness that kept it in place and crawl out of the pile of debris through a tiny hole. Thomas's sister was found on top of the collapsed roof of the house. The clothes had been stripped from her back by the force of the blast, and the sixteen-year-old was rendered mute for four days by the trauma.

Meanwhile, Eileen Bees was sheltering in the well-used back room of her family home in Clay Lane, in the Stoke area of Coventry. She was among a dozen children who lived with their parents in the three-bedroom house, the youngest of whom was born a year before the outbreak of war. Her father, Thomas Weston, was an army veteran who had spent years in India before returning to his native London and marrying Violet Plowman after the First World War. The couple moved first to Nottingham then Coventry in pursuit of work. A factory worker

on Lockers Lane, Thomas was also a member of the Home
Guard and spent nights on duty, away from home.

One of Eileen's brothers had already left home by that
November and one of her sisters was at a dance, having gone
there straight from work. Too big to fit inside any Anderson
shelter, the family would remain at home during the raids,
cowering in the back room of the house.

Before long, its large sash window was shattered by the
force of a blast at the rear of the property. Terrified, the
family moved to the front room, which was usually only used
at Christmas and Easter. Soon afterwards, a bomb blast at
the front showered them with shards of glass. Eileen was
pulled from the sofa by her older brother William, who was
seventeen, just before a large sheet of glass sheared into the
cushions. At the very least, he had prevented serious injury,
but his quick and instinctive actions probably saved her life.

The house was wrecked. Violet knew it was time to move
her family to somewhere that offered greater protection, but
when she tried to open the front door it was jammed with
rubble. The screams of the children were audible for a few
moments above the shriek of the bombs, which alerted the
Irish lodgers who lived next door.

They rushed to the rescue, dug away the rubble to open
the door and carried the youngest of the children to a nearby
air-raid shelter. On the way, Eileen noticed sparkling glass
on the ground and the redness of the sky, cut through with
searchlights.

Inside the public shelter, there was a woman with her
husband and a budgerigar, a bird that remained remarkably
chirpy throughout the ordeal. A woman with a large leather
coat was there, too, dramatically throwing it like a blanket
across the children when bombs fell close by. Irritated,

Eileen's mother finally asked her not to, fearing that the youngsters would suffocate.

She was not the only one feeling tetchy. Arguments about the number of bombs that were falling and their proximity reared up in the shelter between some of the older men and teenagers who bobbed in to take cover as they made their way across the city to their homes. Despite the nervous tension, everyone was prepared to squeeze together to offer someone a seat in a shelter. At least, in most cases.

Some were unwelcome in public shelters – for example, if their children were poorly. With contagious diseases such as whooping cough and diphtheria commonplace and sometimes proving fatal, those with sick youngsters often did the decent thing and stayed at home. Others simply preferred the privacy of their own four walls.

Like Christina Stephenson, Mary Heath worked at Daimler. Her job was to engrave part numbers on the metalwork that went into bombers. In 1937, aged sixteen, she had come to Coventry with her large family from Bolton, in Lancashire in order to find work after opportunities in the cotton mills began to diminish. She was one of eleven children, four of whom had already died at a young age. The job at Daimler was her second after she had initially worked making radios at GEC.

During the raid, she sheltered in the cupboard under the stairs with her mother. Although she was not suffering from an infectious disease, her mother had diabetes and chose to remain at home. They had used the cupboard for protection before when the siren had sounded and usually managed to find their way into the kitchen to make a cup of tea at some stage, or to use the bathroom upstairs. This time, there was no opportunity to leave the confines of the cupboard. It sounded as though bombs were landing at the back door.

They decided they could manage without a drink and, fortunately, there was a bucket on hand for calls for nature.

As Coventry steeled itself below, the German pilots in the skies above were cold and, in some cases, a bit confused about the nature of their target. While they were only too delighted to knock out Britain's industrial capability, many were less certain about meting out death and destruction to its citizens. According to *The Luftwaffe Diaries* by Cajus Bekker, one pilot said, 'The usual cheer that greeted a direct hit stuck in our throats. The crew just gazed down on the sea of flames in silence. Was this really a military target?'

However, all of those who were airborne were concerned with the sub-zero temperatures that permeated even the thickest flying jacket. One Nazi war correspondent, who accompanied a crew, wrote:

> The cold at the height at which we flew was murderous. Our airmen were frozen stiff and could not have borne it much longer even though the whole flight lasted less than an hour …
>
> The anti aircraft barrage was fierce and planes were caught on numerous occasions by searchlights but were able to escape each time.

One propaganda piece, credited to Ju 88 aircrew member Carl Henze, failed to mention the cold and focused more on the glory of the night when he circled the city before departing for Germany.

> The streets of the doomed city are bright as day below. Thick clouds of smoke conceal the damage and climb ever higher over the industrial district. Here and there

are high, almost smokeless fires. The black of the night has vanished. The flyers see a terrible but beautiful picture of the most modern weapons of destruction. What a peculiar thought that only a few hours ago, activity filled those buildings that now lie in soot and ashes! Albion, that is what you wanted!

What the flyers see is indescribable! It is impossible to describe all the details of an industrial city burning in every corner! The flat clouds that are still at about 3,000 metres have taken on a reddish tinge, here a bit more red, there more grey-red. Hundreds of fires add to the unforgettable picture. Searchlights and flares still shine, almost invisible in the light of the fires. In the distance, new flashes are visible as further attack waves hit their targets.

# Chapter Seven

## 'The yellow and purple colours of the flames were just like crocuses'

*A Coventry Fireman*

Outside, it was as one witness said, 'a first hand view of hell'. However, not everyone was either in a shelter or seeking one. One aggrieved factory worker was roaming the shattered streets of Coventry, navigating cratered roads and blazes as tall as houses with difficulty. He passed the time of day with a frantic fireman, cursing the raid as 'this bloody lot' because it would make him late for work.

At Coventry Climax, incendiary bombs kept falling and Len Dacombe was constantly racing around his section with buckets of sand, trying to suffocate fires before they could spread. He turned away after dousing one that landed on the duckboard which covered the factory floor, thinking he had put it out, when it exploded. He was thrust forward by the blast but was not injured. As he glanced back, he saw the incendiary bomb flare up and, like Dr Winter, Len thought fleetingly of Christmas. Soon after that, a string of four bombs fell into the factory. One hit the boring machine, the second a milling machine and a third destroyed the sprinkler stop valve. As water spurted from the mangled sprinkler system and began flooding the floor, Len found his way to the wheel that controlled the valve by the flickering light of flames outside. Like everyone else, Len was dog-tired from working twelve-hour shifts in the factory and performing his duties as a special constable. Even so, he found the strength to turn the valve sufficiently to stop the gush of water. By now, he was working alongside six of the works' firemen.

The fourth bomb had hit a girder in the roof and broken its fins before landing on a pile of camshafts. Although the camshafts were shattered by the impact, the bomb lay inert where it came to rest. Tentatively, Len touched it and found his fingers covered in pungent grease. He and his fellow firefighters retreated to the brick shelter as another string of seven bombs fell on the factory and hit the ground tens of yards away. He was not given to fear, but even Len held his breath as he felt one of the bombs tunnelling through the concrete beneath his feet. Had it exploded, he would have been killed – becoming one of the Coventry Blitz statistics. He breathed once more when he realised it was a second delayed action bomb, designed to explode later rather than immediately; it was later dealt with by army explosives experts during daylight hours.

Len had so far escaped injury. But not everyone in Coventry was so fortunate and the hospital was swamped with casualties. Before the raid, stretcher-bearers had set out a hundred trestle tables at the hospital in readiness to receive the injured as part of an emergency planning procedure. Very soon it was clear they would not be sufficient, given the number of dazed patients coming through the doors. Many had blast injuries, a few had survived with gruesome wounds after being struck by shrapnel hurtling through the air, while others had been picked up by the force of an explosion and tossed against walls or roads. All were caked in thick dust.

John Sargent began assessing patients, some of whom were standing, while others slumped wearily in the long line that was forming. He and his co-worker Doug Henderson undid hastily applied tourniquets on bomb-shattered limbs. Using saline solution, they cleaned the smutty faces and soothed the gritty eyes lined up in front of them.

There was no sense of panic. John and his fellow ambulance crews had been put through their paces on numerous practice runs, and now that the disaster was happening for real, there was simply no time to break stride. As for the patients, they were numb with shock. Many had seen their houses collapse, or witnessed family and friends dead beside them. The sound of close explosions was still ringing in their ears.

John had been working swiftly and on autopilot when he brought in the body of a little girl from an ambulance.

Aged about four, she bore no apparent injuries. Her eyes were closed, her cheeks just slightly puffed. At first glance, she seemed to be soundly asleep in his arms. In fact, she was dead. Almost instantly, John recognised that the force of a blast had burst her lungs. For a moment, John was transfixed. His mind went back a dozen years to the time when his sister Joan had died of diphtheria. She too had been about four, sweet and shy. She bore an uncanny resemblance to the girl who now lay inert in his embrace.

Before Joan's death, the two had been inseparable, romping around the countryside and being brought to book by their fearsome father when he believed they were shirking their chores. Although she was christened Joan, her nickname among the family was 'Happy'. The day she died, John felt that his childhood had ended. His mother never recovered from the loss. She had worn black from that day to this and a smile had rarely visited her face again. Instinctively, John had known he would have to look after his mother when her will to live evaporated with the light in her only daughter's eyes. He had also been devastated by Joan's death.

A doctor's sharp request for aid brought him back to the present.

In a split second, the glimpse of the Berkshire countryside bathed in sunlight and ringing with children's laughter which he saw in his mind's eye was replaced by the grey, shuffling ranks of Blitz victims and the hoarse sound of cries and coughing. The Blitz had been in progress for about two hours. Blinking back the tears for the first and last time that night, he gently laid the little girl down behind a screen and made his way to one of three theatres on the hospital's first floor.

At about the same time, the first high-explosive bomb to hit the St John Ambulance Brigade headquarters fell, blowing doors off. Five minutes later, another brought the roof down in one of the garages. Although telephone lines were disrupted, the base still had contact with central control, the fire station and the hospital. That was how news reached the division controller that ambulances were suffering from punctures caused by shattered glass all over the roads. Spare tyres were sent out while stocks lasted.

Two more bombs isolated the building and all the exits were blocked. When the telephone lines finally fell silent, the St John ambulances congregated at the police station instead.

As a six-year-old, Alan Edgson was terrified by the incessant bombing: 'It was a bit like being pinned to a dartboard while some bloke with a blindfold on was throwing darts at you. You expect every one to hit you.'

Jean Taylor was celebrating becoming a teenager at her home in Holbrooks when the raid began. A chorus of 'Happy Birthday' had only just finished when the first explosions boomed and, with the raid starting so early, her family guessed it would be a difficult night ahead. She spent the night in a shelter at a school with several hundred others: 'I was sitting there between my sister, who was really upset, and my brother-in-law who'd come back from Dunkirk shell-shocked.

'The most frightening thing was the ack-ack noise of the guns.

'I remember saying to God that I just wanted to make it to fourteen.'

There was talk before and after the raid of evacuating, but her father would have none of it, saying 'We live together as a family and we die together as a family'.

One boy who had been sent out of Coventry for his own safety suffered a different kind of torment that night as he saw the city burning from a distance. At the farm where he and his brother were living, he stood grimly watching the attack in safety but knowing that their parents were at its heart: 'It was like standing in heaven, looking at hell. It was a week before we knew mother and father were quite well.'

At post 607, Alan Hartley had returned after dousing a series of incendiaries to find an emergency unfolding. Like others around Coventry, his colleagues were encountering the incendiary devices that flared up shortly after hitting the ground, catching fire fighters unawares. The sting in the tail, the explosive cap that showered the surroundings with white-hot phosphorous metal, injured the men because they had never experienced it before. The device caused anguish everywhere that night, not least to the post's head warden, who suffered face, arm and leg injuries. He had been brought back to the ARP post and urgently needed medical attention.

Earlier that evening, Alan had spotted a mobile anti-aircraft gun moving into position in Grayswood Avenue.

What he did not realise was that they had brought down the telephone wires with one of their first shells. Now there was no way of making contact with the ambulance service. There was only one thing for it and Alan knew exactly what to do, thanks to the training he had received. Quickly, he made ready to ride into the city to get help.

There was some consternation among the remaining adult ARP staff who told him, 'It's not safe out there.' Indeed, the ground was shaking with the impact of the bombs dropping on the city centre little more than a mile away. But a quick glance around the post told him that there was no one better suited to the task than himself.

'I'm going,' he called out as he made for the door. The hubbub of babble and bombing drowned out any further objections. Grabbing his cycle, he pedalled as fast as he as could towards the blazing city centre. Although there was a strict ban on using lights outside, there was already a sufficient number of fires to illuminate his journey.

The sky ahead of him was continually swept by searchlights, swinging from one direction to the next in pursuit of German aeroplanes. Every so often, one would catch a glimpse of distant metal in its mighty light – it looked like a giant moth momentarily transfixed in a powerful torch beam. Other searchlights sited around the city rushed to unite with the first. Then another string of explosions erupted, and a further volley of anti-aircraft shells fired by way of response.

Despite the proximity of enemy aeroplanes and lumps of flying shrapnel, Alan kept cycling towards the city. If he had felt afraid, there were numerous bolt-holes he could have sought in which to sit out the raid. But there was only one task on his mind – getting help for the warden – and fears for his own safety were pushed away with every turn of the pedals.

Near the centre, he headed towards Smithford Street and the Council House where Alan knew he could make a call for help. However, the narrow street had been holed by an enormous bomb. Alan peered over the jagged edge of the shattered road. At the bottom of the crater some 30ft below were the waters of the River Sherbourne. This underground stretch of waterway usually wound its way peacefully and unseen beneath the road. Now, it was like a mirror, reflecting the flames that were engulfing the city.

Desperately, Alan looked around for a way past and saw a 2-foot-wide section of pavement on the right-hand side that was wonky but which had not yet collapsed. That was his path. He hauled his bicycle on to his shoulder, pulled his tin hat down on his head, swung his gas mask case across his stomach and began edging his way across the parapet bridging the side of the crater.

Soon he was back in the saddle, but his progress was repeatedly slowed by piles of debris strewn across the red-hot road. The bicycle was again slung across his shoulder as he slithered among the masonry. Woolworths was on fire, as was Marks & Spencer opposite. Flames were arcing to cover some of the roads at the heart of the firestorm that was gripping the city.

As he passed the Arcade, its glass roof shattered and thunderously collapsed. He turned towards Broadgate, only to feel a burning hot wind that was blowing up the street from the direction of the cathedral wash over him.

At the cathedral, a number of fires were already melding together, although thankfully, those who had initially sought refuge from the raid in the crypt had long since hurried away. Firefighters found themselves unable to help as the roof blazed uncontrollably due to its flawed design. Incendiaries lodged with ease on one part of the roof, which was almost flat. Immediately beneath, there was a highly flammable inner skin made of oak, poised to net further incendiaries as they penetrated the damaged outer roof. So at a lofty height the blaze raged, out of reach and out of control.

A decision had been taken before the raid not to paint the word '*Kirche*' – German for church – on the roof, as it would probably not been seen by enemy pilots. However, a plan to cover the cathedral roof with earth to help stifle incendiaries was also rejected in case the fabric of the building was damaged. This strategy might have helped preserve the building's skeleton – although the volume of ordnance would probably have been too great for the soil to work effectively.

Built mostly in the fourteenth and fifteenth centuries, St Michael's had already been damaged by an incendiary bomb that had fallen through the inner roof during an air raid on 14 October, causing a thousand pounds' worth of damage.

Four people, including the Provost Dick Howard, who had spent all evening doing their best to conquer the flames, must have wondered if more and better defences should have been installed. By 8.00 p.m., the chancel roof, south aisle, nave and the top of three chapels were ablaze. Wooden cathedral furniture helped to feed the fires. When another group of fires erupted from incendiaries, the Provost, the stonemason Jock Forbes and two younger men, were hampered by failing supplies of sand and water, and individually, their strength was ebbing away. They became aware of the sound of dripping, molten lead from the smoke-shrouded roof.

Fighting the fire seemed to be a lost cause, so they joined teams of men who rushed in to save valuable ornaments that were plucked from the cathedral and taken to the nearby police station, which remained undamaged. Religious books, altar crosses, candlesticks and the colours of the Royal Warwickshire regiment were among the items rescued. Fortunately, the medieval stained-glass had been removed from the cathedral the previous year as a precaution.

With every passing minute, they hoped that the fire brigade would respond to their emergency call. But the city's firefighters were embroiled in a battle on a broad front, with similarly limited supplies. At 9.30 p.m., a crew of Solihull firemen finally arrived at the vestry door. Lengths of hose were put in place around the cathedral in a bid to save it, but before the operation could start in earnest, the water ran out. Any hopes of getting water high enough to douse the roof top blazes were finally dashed.

Silent observers watched as the roofs of the Children's Chapel and the Lady Chapel eventually collapsed onto their respective pews. Elaborate interior woodwork also fell victim to the flames, as did the elegant organ, once played by Handel. There was a brief glimmer of hope at about 10.00 p.m., when the water came on again after another hydrant was tapped, but the pressure was too low to make a difference and that also soon turned into a dribble.

Suddenly, a loud crash caught the attention of everyone near the cathedral. No one knew if it was the sound of the main roof collapsing as steel girders added during a nineteenth-century refurbishment buckled, or a high explosive coming to ground.

The firemen finally withdrew at 11.00 p.m., unable to save the historic joinery or masonry. They joined the provost and his helpers in watching the slow death of the grand and well-loved building, the only cathedral to be destroyed in Britain during the Second World War. Before midnight – and hours before the raid came to an end – only the tower, spire, an outer wall and the bronze effigy and tomb of Coventry's first bishop, Huyshe Wolcott Yeatman-Biggs, remained.

Elsewhere, factory fire tenders manned by volunteer firemen who worked in tandem with the national service had taken to the city streets in force. The men with Rootes Fire Service, based in Humber Park, responded to a call made at 8.10 p.m. to help tackle the blaze at Owen Owen, Coventry's sole department store. Realising that it was beyond control, they went to Hales Street, intending to pump water from the River Sherbourne. Another brigade was already deployed in the burning shell of Corporation Street, so both teams worked together, with the Rootes men tackling the flames at Warico Fireplace shop and Anslow's, which sold second-hand furniture. A daunting task was made hopeless as bombs and debris continually made holes in their hoses and fractured gas mains also ignited.

'At the same time a lot of incendiaries came scuttling down from one end of Hales Street to the old fire station. It looked like a spring garden – the yellow and purple colours of the flames were just like crocuses,' said one fireman. 'Anyway, we'd just put Anslow's fire out and these bombs struck it up again.'

A machine operator at Alvis Mechanisation, who spent his nights with the works fire brigade, was blown into Burton's Menswear in the city centre. 'The blast was so great that it split my trousers all up the middle,' he said later. 'I was tempted to help myself to a pair from Burton's. I was in dire necessity but thought better of it. There were harsh penalties for looting.'

Some people were quick to help the firemen where they could. The landlord of the Queen's Head told them, 'Any beer you can find lads, take it out and have it.' Consequently, some fire tenders returned with barrels attached. Other bystanders led firemen to safety after they were temporarily blinded by the glare of the flames. Everyone in the city centre had to move fast to sidestep a river of burning butter escaping from the Maypole Dairy.

Auxiliary fireman Sydney Smith, who worked at the Armstrong Whitworth factory during the day, was getting used to going round the clock with very little sleep. But on the night of the Blitz, the cold weather made life even more difficult than usual.

'It was so cold that night I found that I was frozen to the pavement on one occasion.

'We had gone on duty at 7.00 p.m. and were still damping down at 8.00 a.m. the following morning – we never even heard the "All Clear" at all.'

There is little doubt that most men driving cars and tenders through corridors of fire and wrestling with hoses served by an uncertain water supply drew on enormous reserves of inner courage. Some of the most exemplary performances were later recognised with honours.

Control officer Campbell Kelly was given a George Medal for his work. It was not the first time he had displayed conspicuous bravery, either. Kelly already had to his credit a Military Medal that he had won at Passchendaele and a Military Cross, the latter earned in 1918 when he held a post under enemy fire while suffering the effects of a gas attack. He was also the recipient of a Croix de Guerre after serving with the French Fifth Army.

Kelly went on to work with the intelligence division of the British Army in Ireland when the fight for independence was at full throttle. A regular interrogator of IRA prisoners, he became a target for reprisals and survived an assassination attempt. In 1923, as a lieutenant in the Royal Garrison Artillery, he was made an Order of the British Empire, further recognition of a distinguished career. However, just five years later, he was dismissed from the service after a court martial following accusations of financial impropriety, the details of which remain unclear.

Like other Irish men, Kelly presumably came to Coventry in the Thirties to secure work, and in 1939, he married for a second time. His George Medal was presented to him in 1941, with a citation that revealed how he had led a team that saved a factory from destruction before joining forces with the city fire service. On his return, he helped dig out the bodies of policemen buried by a high explosive. His first officer David Lloyd was awarded an OBE.

Hero though he undoubtedly was, there remained something of the maverick about Kelly. Later the same year, Kelly appeared in court, charged with bigamy. He had married in Coventry without getting a divorce from the woman he had wed in 1917, who was the mother of his five children. His marital duplicity did not dampen the respect that many felt for him. When he died from kidney problems in 1942, a fire officer said, 'He did marvellous work in every raid and was a man completely without nerves.'

Chief Fire Officer George Collier, of the Humber works brigade, also got a George Medal – recognition of his bravery for continuing to fight fires inside a factory building that had taken three direct hits. He had already had a narrow escape after directing a hose from the roof of a building that collapsed beneath him. Although he injured his back, he refused to seek help until the raid ended.

The records of those who received George Medals still exist; a window of fleeting clarity on mayhem and chaos of that night.

At Alfred Herbert Ltd, Eddie Hunt was praised for his gallantry in helping the city fire brigade, as was Arthur Ward, for rescuing people trapped under burning houses in Lythalls Lane, and George Brownless, who also helped to fight a fire there. When Brownless was injured, William Simpson took his place, displaying an equally cool and effective leadership. Despite a pelvis injury, Walter Selby, a fireman at the factory, crawled from its control room to the Holmsdale Road police station to plead for help for a man with a serious lung injury and for more firefighters.

Leading fireman Joseph Brown was left unconscious after one blast. But when he came round he insisted on continuing his job. And when an incendiary fell on one of the vehicles towing a fire tender, he leapt in to drive it to a hose so that the fire could be extinguished. Messenger Derek Durbridge was blown across a street by the force of a bomb as he guided a crew to the scene of a call-out. He was buried by debris, but eventually managed to free himself from the rubble and reported for duty at the Central Fire Station, only to be caught up once again in a blast shortly afterwards. Both men were later awarded the Order of the British Empire, along with two regular firemen, John Boissonade and Norman Brown, and another auxiliary, William Maddocks. Their joint citation reads:

> They were responsible for an extremely efficient and intricate system of relaying water in the centre of the City, as a result of which the spread of fire in this highly congested area was checked at many points. Between them they rallied and encouraged crews whose endurance was severely taxed. In movements of men

and appliances they employed skill and resource for which previous experience had set no standards to act as a guide. Their cheerfulness and absolute disregard of personal safety were [sic] outstanding.

It was not only firemen who were recognised with honours. Marjorie Perkins, who was a nurse at Messrs Pattison and Hobourn Ltd in Cash's Lane, continued helping casualties at the works, in nearby streets and in public shelters long after she was due to have finished her shift. Twice, she suffered injuries herself; she was flung across the surgery by a blast in which she sustained internal wounds, and she was left unconscious by a second explosion. Nurse Perkins was awarded the George Medal with a citation that read: 'Throughout the night she did her work with utter disregard for her own personal safety; her courage and devotion to the injured under the most trying circumstances were outstanding. Since that time she has had to remain under the care of her own doctor.'

Awards were made and medals presented properly to recognise uncommon acts of courage. However, there is an argument to say that every fireman facing the uncertain threat of blazes as a result of aerial assault, and all those who tended the injured in perilous conditions without regard for their own safety, were worthy of celebration.

As the night wore on, the waves of bombers seemed relentless. Firemen from across the region and auxiliaries from all over Coventry were in action. In addition to crews from the city, there were fifty firefighters from Leeds, forty-eight men from London and fifty-two from Bristol as well as one crew and a pump each from Kenilworth, Bedworth, Rugby, Leamington, Stratford and Nuneaton plus four from Birmingham.

The men from Stratford lost the big car that they used to tow their fire tenders, affectionately called 'the flying bedstead', after it was buried by rubble. When they returned home, they were as 'black as coal, as if they had been dumped in a river and put up a chimney', according to the wife of one. They were also reluctant to talk about what they had seen. According to one fireman who came from Stratford-upon-Avon, sixty-five firefighters died that night, although official figures vary.

One crew that tried to save Sylvester's Jewellers in Cross Cheaping was showered with glass as a bomb blew out a plate-glass window. Then, the crew members were buried in the rubble of a building as it collapsed.

At the Central Fire Station, telephones had been ringing continuously until water poured through the ceiling, causing the electricity to short circuit. Switchboard operators were finally forced to evacuate in a hail of sparks. After the telephones went dead, the only communication between fire crews was carried out by messengers, unless anyone had reason to report in person. One of the messengers was the son of Bill Kimberley, a city fireman killed outside Coventry and Warwickshire Hospital. He asked the whereabouts of his father, but was not told what happened until some time later.

Bill Kimberley was among numerous people who died in the line of duty that night.

A father of two, Jack Eaves was an auxiliary fireman with British Thomson-Houston who helped the city firemen with the company's trailer pump. He left them, busy and imperilled, to return to the works to retrieve more equipment. In the few minutes he was there, a bomb fell and killed him.

Seven men in Alfred Herbert's works fire brigade died together. The youngest, Peter Robbins, the son of a squadron leader, was just sixteen years old. Frank Richardson and Edward Brown were nineteen years old. Another nineteen-year-old, Dennis Brown, died alongside them – just hours before his brother Eddie, who was three years younger, also perished.

It seems that Eddie had heard about the tragedy at Alfred Herbert's and, using a borrowed bicycle, pedalled to Stoney Stanford Swimming Baths in the hope of finding his brother among the survivors. While he was there, the baths took a direct hit and he was killed.

Meanwhile, two auxiliary firemen were among the dead at Rover's Helen Street plant, and there were losses, too, among the ARP units working to keep the civilian population safe.

Doris Lampitt, aged forty-five, was on duty as an ARP warden outside Crampers Field air-raid shelter when she was killed. Alongside her civil defence duties she also ran a wool shop. Another ARP warden, Walter Phillips, helped to release four people buried in the rubble of their bombed home. A fifth was still trapped and Mr Phillips, a machine-shop superintendent at British Thomson-Houston, stayed to give first aid. He was killed, along with his patient, when a land mine fell on them. (His widow and two children were also made homeless that night.)

The war had already taken its toll on the ranks of the police force and the specials who assisted them. Sergeant James Fox, aged thirty-seven, and PC William Leedham, aged thirty-six, died on 12 October 1940 while evacuating the area surrounding a delayed action bomb. Nine days later, Special Constable William Sinclair was killed during a raid.

On the night of the Blitz, two police officers, two police messengers and four special constables perished, as well as a police war reserve constable, Frederick Strong, who succumbed to his wounds three days after he was injured. One of the policemen was Ken Rollins, who was aged thirty. He was with his best friend, Ted Bloomfield, whose wife Mary later recorded what happened in a powerful diary entry written at the end of the war. She did not include the terrible details in the entries relating to the Blitz: '[At the end of the war Ted remembered] the bomb that threw him against the council house walls, killing his best friend Ken Rollins who was going to help get people out of the debris in Much Park Street, flinging [Ken's] large body over the wall of the Miss Patricks' shop where his colleagues were forced to stand by and watch him burn.'

The other policeman was William Timms, who was twenty-three. One of the specials, twenty-six-year-old William Lambe, died trying to help those trapped in a collapsed shelter. Police messenger Thomas Lowry was sixteen when he was killed, while fellow messenger Bertram West was seventeen.

Yet, it is the story of survivors, especially those who emerged with honour, that are most commonly recounted today. Their actions were committed to record, while hundreds of others who were equally heroic passed into the blur of history without ever imparting their tales. Among serried ranks of heroes, one special constable stood out for his conduct that night.

Special Sergeant Brandon Moss, who worked as a fitter at Armstrong Siddeley, was on duty from 11.00 p.m., and witnessed some of the worst of the bombing. A house in Clay Lane, in Stoke, was one of many flattened by a bomb. Four people were trapped inside. Moss dug a tunnel to them, oblivious to the dangers of falling bombs, fast-flying shrapnel and a fractured gas main. He managed to lead three of the people to safety through the small opening, the fourth occupant having already died. He then brought someone else out alive from another collapsed home nearby, where three people were killed.

A matter of metres away, lodged in a pub doorway, a delayed action bomb lay in ominous silence. No one knew when it would explode. Despite the threat, Moss continued to tunnel into wreckage. His actions earned him the George Cross, the highest gallantry award that can be made to civilians.

At the post office, assistant engineer Gilbert Griffiths was battling to keep communications operational, a crucial task that would later be recognised with the presentation of a George Medal. It should have been his night off, but he had already taken to his bicycle and ridden through the bombing raid to reach the post office which he could see was at risk.

While telephone lines were brought down by artillery fire and bombs, the telegraph system, which kept Coventry in touch with London and other major cities, could still function. With two colleagues, William Williams and John Wilkins, who were also honoured with OBEs, Griffiths helped to restore severed communications and kept them working until dawn.

When fire eventually reached the post office, the three fought the blaze themselves. The smoke proved too much for Mr Williams, who collapsed and was hauled to safety by the other two. Eventually, the fire brigade arrived to help.

Thanks to the communications system, help was at least directed to Coventry.

George Medals also went to a nineteen-year-old ARP warden, a clerk by day, who helped dig out seven people from a buried Anderson shelter, and a thirty-two-year-old doctor attached to the Barkers Butts School First Aid Post who, 'while fires were raging and bombs falling, coolly continued to go … on foot and … by bicycle from one incident to another administering morphia … and applying first aid'.

If the raid on Coventry proved anything, it was that a group of diverse people bound by a common aim could give an excellent account of themselves even in the face of appalling punishment, not for medals or money – or even personal survival. The courage and compassion that was exhibited that night seemed to be written somewhere in their DNA.

# Chapter Eight

# 'With such continuous fire we had visions of running out of ammunition'

*Donald Lee, Anti-aircraaft Gunner on the night of the Coventry Blitz*

Luck seemed to play a part in deciding who lived and who died.

One man was so concerned about the fate of his pregnant wife that he persuaded a friend in his twenties to drive him home. Soon after they set off from The Greyhound public house in Much Park Street, where the young driver lived, a bomb fell in front of the car and left a crater in the road. Although the prospective father was dazed, he survived, but the driver who was doing him a good turn died.

At least one family left their home for the shelter and died there, while their empty house remained intact. Another family was divided forever by a decision made in the heat of the raid. After their house was destroyed in a blast, they sought shelter with a neighbour. The father of the family and his young son were killed by falling debris as they approached the neighbour's door. The mother, who had already got to the kitchen and was talking to the owner of the house, survived although her hair caught fire. The woman she was talking to lost an eye.

Some people endured treks under fire between shelters, often escorted by wardens, trying to escape from badly affected areas. But there was little or no communication across the city. To leave one shelter for another was a decision taken on whim or intuition.

One woman decided to stay at home in the raid because her twelve-year-old son was ill and together they sheltered under the stairs. They were killed when the house was destroyed by a bomb blast and her husband, an ARP warden, and another son, who was in the Home Guard, returned after spending the night in the midst of the action to find no trace of their loved ones. Yet, a twelve-year-old girl, who had been having piano lessons with two spinsters, rushed home after the Blitz began even though the women begged her to stay. She survived the night with her family, while the women died after their home was bombed.

For some there seemed to be little luck running in their favour that night. Phyllis Smith, who was twenty-eight, died when the air-raid shelter she was in was blown up. Her father, Arthur, was dug out alive and rushed to Coventry and Warwickshire hospital by ambulance. However, the vehicle also took a direct hit and everyone inside was killed. A couple whose shop was in Coventry city centre went into their cellar to shelter from the bombs. When an explosion fractured a nearby water main the cellar flooded, and when the deluge came into contact with the cellar's electricity supply, they were both electrocuted.

For others fate dealt a more random hand. Two women sheltering in the cellar below their city-centre shop were freed by PC Ted Bloomfield and other rescuers. One of the women was alive but the other who lay a few feet away was dead. An unnamed fire watcher from Alfred Herberts, who joined the works rescue squad when the office roof he was perched on was in danger of collapse, was made an OBE, a fact celebrated in the company magazine. However, fortune did not favour Alexander MacArthur, in the St John Ambulance Brigade division that was also based at Alfred Herbert. He was extinguishing an incendiary near St Nicholas's Church in Radford when he was caught in the blast of a high explosive with three others and died.

One man took advantage of a lull in the air raid and dashed from an air-raid shelter to his house to put the kettle on. In that short distance, he was killed by a bomb, although there was not a mark on his body. His brother-in-law who had accompanied him was unscathed.

In a reversal of fortunes a factory warden escaped with his life after leaving a surface shelter to make a cup of tea. Moments later, the shelter was flattened by a bomb, leaving no survivors. There were deaths and at least one story of survival at the Astoria cinema in Albany Road as well during the raid. One of those who died was a woman with a baby in her arms. Cinemas provided an intoxicating mixture of propaganda and escapism during the war and remained popular venues even during air raids. Staff advised people to leave after the air-raid warning was flashed on the screen, but could not make them. That night, five people perished in the auditorium, while the usherette, who lay prostrate on the floor, lived.

One woman was in Gulson Road Hospital giving birth to her son as the raid raged around her. The Anderson shelter that she would have used in Longfellow Road took a direct hit. Another man had a lucky escape when he went into the central police station to ask for some tea and cigarettes for the policemen and wardens digging out people after an explosion in Dun Cow Yard. As he returned, he saw a bomb kill the people that he had been trying to help. Hysterical from the horror that he had witnessed, he returned to the police station, where he was given peremptory treatment from an officer who had no time for panicky behaviour, no matter how justified the circumstances.

Some people were left tortured by the cruel nature of chance that accompanied aerial bombardment. Trapped in the ruins of one bombed home was eleven-year-old Jeanne Trickett, who had been sheltering with her parents and her sister. She came round from unconsciousness trying to claw the rubble away from her face and rid her mouth of a foul taste. 'I was trying to shout. I heard my father say, that is my little nipper. That was the last words I ever heard him say. He died during the night from his injuries,' she recalled later. When sooty-faced rescuers finally tunnelled in and dragged her out, she begged them not to dirty her hair, which had been newly washed. Both her legs were broken. She kept asking where her parents were and only later was she told that both of them were dead.

And there were some who were blessed with lucky breaks. Raymond Harris, a private in the St John Ambulance Brigade, drove his car into a bomb crater as he made his way to its headquarters. Although dazed by the accident, he spent the rest of the night driving an ambulance until it was put out of action – only later reflecting on this fortunate fluke.

Land girl Margaret Chifney – who had already crashed a tractor into the pond at the farm where she worked – also enjoyed some good fortune that night, though it did not seem so to her at the time. She was at a dance hosted by the YMCA in Coventry with other land girls and soldiers from a local unit. Margaret had been told about living under Blitz

ABOVE: The internal framework for double decker buses was being produced by Daimler factory workers in Coventry in 1938. © *Motoring Picture Library / Alamy*

LEFT: Flight Sgt David Meikle died on British soil after his Stirling bomber crash landed on 12 October 1943, the first of three brothers to die in the conflict. © *Janice Chapman*

LEFT: After being blitzed Coventry became a focus for international tributes. Here wounded American servicemen gather in the ruined cathedral on 13 May 1945 for a Mother's Day service. © *Popperfoto/ Getty Images*

BELOW: After working during night raids, Coventry fire fighters had to stay alert during daylight hours too as blazes continued to flare inside bomb-hit buildings. © *Hulton-Deutsch Collection/ Corbis*

ABOVE: Eileen Bees on the left, with sisters Sylvia, Olive and Dorothy. They were among seven girls and five boys in a family too large for an air raid shelter in the back garden. © *Eileen Bees*

LEFT: According to her daughter, Phyllis Meikle remained remarkably upbeat despite the loss of three sons, feeling fond camaraderie with other women who were also grieving. © *Janice Chapman*

ABOVE: After being a special constable in Coventry before the blitz, Len Dacombe gained first aid training with the Saint John Ambulance Brigade after moving to Oswestry in Shropshire. © *Cecilia Dacombe*

ABOVE: Streets of residential houses on the outskirts of Coventry were also reduced to blackened shells by German bombing. © *Central Press/Getty Images*

ABOVE: Ormiston and Phyllis Meikle kept their grief hidden, despite the scale of their loss. None of their sons lived to see a 25th birthday. © *Janice Chapman*

ABOVE: After the blitz Dennis Adler remained part of the St John Ambulance Brigade in Coventry and was soon an ambulance driver. © *Dennis Adler*

ABOVE: Colin, Ian and David Meikle with sister April as children. © *Janice Chapman*

ABOVE: After the November blitz roads at the centre of the rubble-strewn city were patrolled by soldiers and policemen, dispatched there to help keep the peace. © *ullsteinbild / TopFoto*

ABOVE: When Len and Cecilia got married at Earlsdon in Coventry they walked through an arch of splints held aloft by Cecilia's first aid colleagues.
© *Cecilia Dacombe*

RIGHT: The Dacombes were married for more than 70 years before Len's death in 2013 aged 96.
© *From the collection of Cecilia Dacombe*

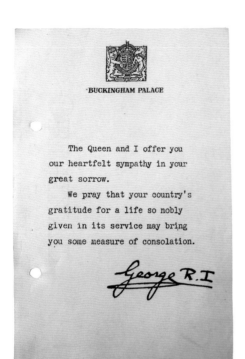

The Queen and I offer you
our heartfelt sympathy in your
great sorrow.

We pray that your country's
gratitude for a life so nobly
given in its service may bring
you some measure of consolation.

*George R.I*

LEFT: After the death of her brother, Eileen's family received a letter of condolence from the King. © *Eileen Bees*

BELOW: Coventry people were surprised and delighted by a hastily organised visit of King George VI with Home Secretary Herbert Morrison, intended to boost morale. © *Fox Photos/Getty Images*

ABOVE: Colin Meikle (middle, back row), died in India a month after peace had been declared in Europe but prior to the end of hostilities in the far east. © *Janice Chapman*

LEFT: As the War continued other cities were destroyed by aerial bombardment just as Coventry had been, including Dresden in Germany shortly before the end of the conflict. © *Sovfoto/UIG via Getty Images*

conditions in London by her father and her sister, a factory worker, who had stayed in the family home in the capital while Margaret went to the countryside to help bring in the wartime harvest. Working at a farm in Hinckley, Margaret had enjoyed having a bedroom of her own and a real bathroom for the first time in her life. When the siren went, she thought that Coventry lay too far inland to be hit by German bombers. But the building she was in caught fire early on and all its occupants were hurried outside by an ARP warden. When she caught sight of the cathedral in flames, Margaret was rooted to the spot even when another series of bombs started to fall. A warden dragged her to the ground, but immediately left her to help a woman who was on fire. He quickly rolled the woman on the ground to put out the flames and then helped her to a shelter, before Margaret had the wherewithal to ask him what to do next.

There was no sign of the girls she had arrived with and she was a stranger in Coventry, with no idea where the nearest public shelter might be.

The moon was like a huge torchlight and the roads had ice on them. The trees were sparkling with frost.

I heard another screaming bomb and threw myself behind a hedge and a short wall and covered my ears against the bang. I don't know how long I stayed [like that], it seemed like hours. There were so many buildings burning now the firemen were helping people rather than trying to put the flames out.

I knew if I didn't move soon I would die from cold, how I wished I had my old breeches and boots on instead of a dress and these silly shoes. How could I run in those?

Margaret decided to make for the station in the hope that she could leave Coventry and find her way home. Walking and running in turns, she set off in the direction of the railways until she looked up and saw a parachute with what looked like a dustbin dangling beneath making its way gently towards her. She jumped behind a wall and covered her ears – but when there was no explosion she resumed her treacherous journey, with the strong feeling that she was making a series of wrong turns.

> After what seemed like hours I saw the railway bridge and I thought "at last" and then, for the second time that night, I was dragged to the ground, this time by a fireman. He said something and pointed to the railway and hanging there like a chandelier was the landmine. The parachute was caught on the bridge.
>
> I spent the rest of the night wet, cold and very frightened in a lady's coal cellar under her house. There were several other occupants. One poor lady had completely lost her mind. She was screaming and trying to get out, saying her son was in the city.

The next day, Margaret returned to the farm where she worked by a combination of car, tractor and horse and cart. Once there, she collapsed on her bed and cried herself to sleep. For years, she marvelled that anyone could have survived the conflagration.

Land mines, also known as parachute mines, were used extensively by the Luftwaffe. Originally designed for use at sea, they were effective on land, too, because they exploded at roof-top level, causing extensive damage as the blast travelled laterally and above ground. They came in two sizes. Both were cylindrical and came down to earth at a sedate 40 miles per hour after being released from a plane's bomb hatch, descending beneath a green, imitation silk parachute.

Those seeing this kind of mine for the first time were often confused by the parachute. More than one observer later recalled dashing forward, imagining that they were going to have to wrestle a German who had bailed out of his aircraft. Indeed, two Polish airmen who ran to detain what they thought was a parachutist died in the ensuing explosion, their bodies unmarked but their lungs destroyed by the blast.

ARP Warden Fred Shipp thought the same thing when his eyes tracked a parachute heading earthwards:

> I moved in its direction thinking it was a German bailing out. I thought we would get him if nothing else. As I went towards it the thing exploded. Of course it was a mine. It was said that the Polish airmen based at the Rialto had fired at it.
>
> The blast knocked me down and I lay gasping for breath for how long I have little idea. Eventually I recovered sufficiently to crawl to a surface shelter in Redesdale Avenue. It was crowded but I managed to squeeze in and the pressure of the bodies kept me on my feet.

One nine-year-old girl on the city outskirts was helped up by her father so she could see a landmine floating gracefully towards earth, slipping into the safety of their shelter just before its impact.

Outside the city centre, parachute mines fell at Exhall, Keresley and Allesley. The sight of them reignited fears that Britain was about to be invaded.

Len Dacombe was also tormented by landmines. As he was walking through the factory with his fellow fire watcher at about 1.00 a.m., one exploded in the neighbouring canal. Its force picked them both up and hurled them through the air, down an aisle and towards a factory wall. Len had the wherewithal to put out his hands to stop his face hitting the brickwork. Together, the men landed in a heap on the floor. They suffered bruising rather than broken bones, but the factory did not escape so lightly. The canteen and the test shop were wrecked. Moreover, as parts of the roof and a wall were destroyed, clay from the depths of the canal was plastered over the machines, ultimately doing more extensive damage than the bombs themselves. Asbestos roofing and glass were also strewn over the machinery and the floor. All that remained were the iron girders which marked where the upper limits of the factory building had once been.

When there was a lull in the bombing, the pair decided to survey the factory from the outside. If they thought the gap in the bombardment would be a meaningful one, they were wrong. As the whine of enemy aircraft sounded overhead once more, a quick survey of the sky told them that they did not have long. A string of bombs was heading their way. They dashed towards the nearest air raid shelter for cover.

The factory was not the only building ablaze. Outside, surrounding streets were ablaze. The ARP station and a furniture warehouse on the other side of the canal were being eaten by fire.

At the shelter in Widdrington Road used by factory workers and residents alike the gate man from the works was broadcasting the bad news. 'Everything's on fire, there's nothing left,' he announced to anyone who would listen, oblivious of the panic he would cause. Len spoke sternly to him, asking him to stay quiet for the sake of public calm. Len was not scared, though. A childhood in India had made him robust. His father, Charles Dacombe, had been a staff sergeant in the Royal Army Service Corps and, as a boy, Len had taken the long voyage to India and spent several years on the subcontinent.

In Bangalore his playground was a rift in the ground, presumably caused by an earthquake, where large ants travelled as one in columns a foot wide. His sister Alice, who was seven years older than he, taught him long division by drawing numbers with a stick in the sand. Len became used to hyenas rooting around the dustbins, but he was once shaken to see a mongoose in the house. 'It means there's a snake here,' explained a servant.

A few days later, the tell-tale sign of silver snake scales on the floor of his bedroom proved that one of the reptiles had been lurking close at hand and had shed its skin before leaving.

On one military base in northern India, he was asleep in barrack housing when Afridi tribesmen smothered themselves in cheetah fat to stop the dogs barking and crept into the military base's armoury. As everyone slept, they made off with every last rifle and bullet and spirited them back to Afghanistan.

To Len, the Blitz produced a new set of challenges, but he was determined they would not unduly terrorise him.

However, it was no longer a case of 'the show must go on' at the Hippodrome. Forces sweetheart Betty Driver – who would later find fame as barmaid Betty Turpin in *Coronation Street* – was cowering on the floor of her dressing room with her sister Freda and five-year-old Julie Andrews, the future

Mary Poppins, who was performing as part of a family troupe. Above them, although they did not know it, three stage hands were spending an unscheduled ten-hour shift on the roof throwing off incendiaries to stop the building igniting.

Nearby, Alan Hartley remained unaware of dramas like these unfolding in the smoke-choked city, still intent on the task in hand. But some of the sights he saw that night remained with him for the rest of his life. He passed a bicycle shop a fireman – his face blackened and his eyes rimmed with red – was wrestling with a hose, but no matter how hard he pulled and twisted, no more than a trickle of water emerged from its nozzle. Struck by the futile efforts of the fireman, he was only distracted when he finally reached his destination. Inside the Council House, someone took down details of the crisis at ARP Post 607. Although he was wheezy from smoke inhalation, it did not take long to pass on the information and soon Alan was outside once more, as attention turned to the next in a long line.

The fireman who had hoped to extinguish the flames at the bicycle shop was now sitting on a box with his head in his hands, his yellow oilskins greyed by the smoky atmosphere. By now, in the early hours of the morning, the city's water supplies, which were estimated to be in the region of 21.3 million gallons, had been exhausted. Ironically, most firemen, frustrated by the lack of water, were standing ankle deep in it because bombs had fractured the city's water pipes, allowing the contents to spill out along the roads.

The city's fire hydrants were often covered by rubble when they were needed and although firemen had access to special reservoirs, usually built on factory sites, there were too few to fulfil the requirements that night. The firemen could also use water from swimming pools, but that source, of course, was also limited and one swimming pool was quickly demolished in a blast.

Alan was glad to see that there was help available for firefighters like the exhausted fellow he had passed. A WVS wagon was on hand to provide tea and some stirring support for the rescue squads.

Alan made his way over rubble in a different direction this time, deciding to risk the Birmingham Road on his route home. Ducking under a railway bridge, Alan started when he saw a railway engine teetering on the brink, blown off its rails by the force of a blast. As he headed out of the city, the scenes of destruction diminished. The air was tinged with fumes, but the number of fires was far fewer.

His first stop was Grayswood Avenue, where his mother and sister had spent the night in the shelter. His father Harold had previously returned to Barrow-in-Furness where shipbuilding was once again in full production. Then he made his way back to the post, beaten by an ambulance that had collected the injured head warden. Thanks to Alan, he survived the injuries he sustained that night.

Curiously, the cathedral bells continued to chime long into the night until finally electricity was lost.

At 1.45 a.m. a note from the Home Security's office in Birmingham betrayed a note of panic about the drama unfolding in Coventry:

> Coventry has suffered and is still suffering severe damage from HE, land mines and fires, many fires still raging and already a number of shops, commercial premises and the cathedral have been gutted.
>
> The streets are littered with debris and casualties are likely to be high. Several police officers are known to have

been killed and it is estimated that at least 200 additional police will be required to be drafted into the city.

Throughout, the anti-aircraft guns were firing hard, sometimes wide of the mark, but hoping at least to cause alarm in the cockpits of a passing aeroplane. A lively response from the ack-ack guns also helped to keep up morale during raids.

One diary entry reveals the hopes people were investing in the anti-aircraft guns:

> ... Although we had not heard the sirens we heard planes grunting overhead and soon the guns began to sound. That was 7.30 pm and now it is nearly 10 o'clock and never have we had such a pounding of guns, almost without cessation for over two hours. I only hope we have brought some of them down. Heavens what a bang, the house shook then. I think we could do without any more of this. We certainly have expended some ammunition on these Nazis tonight.

Donald Lee was one of the gunners at Binley, which lies on the outskirts of the city. In April 1939, he joined the Territorials after being a clerk for the Wesleyan and General Assurance Society in Birmingham. He arrived in Coventry, alongside many other Birmingham men, with the 95th Anti Aircraft Royal Artillery. Afterwards, he joined the regular army.

All gunners had been ordered to fire in a concentrated barrage as waves of planes came over. The only breaks that the men had were the short periods between each wave of aeroplanes. As the instruments on the command post were not in use because of the barrage, there were extra helpers to carry ammunition. Lee recalled, 'Although it was a cold night, halfway through the raid the gunners were in their shirt sleeves. With such continuous fire we had visions of running out of ammunition.'

An incendiary bomb dropped on the site and started a fire, but it was quickly put out by men who feared they might be illuminated as a target if the flames took hold.

Actual firing stopped at about 5.30 a.m., but the order to stand down didn't come until 7.15 a.m..

By 3.30 a.m. 200 fires had been reported in Coventry. The mounting crisis was enough to send one chief fire officer with an auxiliary force out of his mind. Every few minutes, he shouted at the top of his voice 'Bombs, bloody great bombs'. He ended up in hospital.

A Civil Defence report written soon after the raid said, 'The attack was incessant and bombs may be said to have "rained in torrents". This made it impossible for a while for the fire service to use either the small Sherbourne River or canals when, owing to damage to the mains, the water from the public services ceased.

'An earthquake could not have rendered the scene more desolate or distressing.'

On the outskirts of Coventry, the raid had far less impact. Marjorie Edge was a ten-year-old sheltering in the family Anderson shelter in Wheelwright Lane, in Holbrooks. She lived there with her parents and her brother, sister and grandfather, who was a retired collier. In common with other children, Marjorie was not unduly fazed by life during wartime. At school, Marjorie's teacher gave the pupils honest assessments of how the conflict was progressing and together they monitored the activities of HMS *Coventry*. In class, the girls knitted while the boys dug the school garden, which provided vegetables for school dinners.

That night, her father William was fire watching and her grandfather typically declined the dubious comforts of the shelter, preferring to keep two elderly neighbours company in their house instead. They could hear the pounding being given to the city, but felt relatively secure in the shelter until a land mine came down at the end of the garden. The main impact of the November Blitz, as far as Marjorie was concerned, was the death of the numerous hens kept by her grandfather, which helped to supplement the family's rations. Her after-school chores had included collecting buckets of peelings from the neighbours to help feed the birds. Although her grandfather was careful to ensure that she never considered the hens as pets, he would not allow her to go to the end of the garden where their bodies were scattered until he had cleared away the remains.

Soon her father, a socialist, would resume his arguments with her grandfather, a staunch Conservative, like other families in the industrial hot spots. Those at the centre of the city were not so fortunate.

Casualties were piling up at the hospital, even though many ambulance men were badly hampered in bringing back patients. A large number had by now abandoned their vehicles, which were beset with punctures, and were making their way around the city on foot.

One ARP officer from Courtaulds was taken to hospital early on after being injured. To his horror, he realised it was at the heart of a square marked by flares and spent an anxious night on the floor, convinced it was going to be destroyed. The raid had already left the hospital without a mains supply of electricity, which went out at about midnight. Fortunately, there were generators on hand to provide essential light and heat.

John Sargent's role in the theatre was grisly, but necessary. It was his job to steady the mangled limbs crushed by masonry as they were being amputated by surgeons.

He did not think about everything the patients had lost that night; rather he thought about the chance of life that was being offered by expert hospital treatment. Doctors and nurses worked calmly and efficiently, even when the floor shook with the force of the last bomb. Later, Dr Harry Winter called the level of morale at the hospital 'stupefying', explaining the difficulties that he and other doctors faced that night when they were confronted with ranks of bomb blast victims:

> We couldn't work very rapidly. Wounds are very tricky in the war of bombs. The complication with bomb lacerations is that there is a small wound on the surface but extensive disruption underneath.
>
> Everything is pulped together. It's no use fixing the surface wound without doing a major cutting job on the inside – and that takes time.

As long as there was some power – even from a dim bulb – the doctors and nurses were determined to tend the endless stream of patients. As John Sargent examined the faces of the medical staff, frozen in concentration, he marvelled at the way they barely flinched at the whistles and loud bangs that filled the air. Although the bombs were startling and fell in close by, the surgeons' hands remained steady. Nurses who might in different circumstances shriek at sudden sounds maintained an icy calm.

After several hours in the theatre, he suddenly became aware of the heat. His body was encased in the mandatory heavy-duty Civil Defence uniform and sweat was pouring down his back and legs as he moved swiftly between operating table and disposal bin. For four hours, medical staff continued with emergency operations. Supplies of blood at the hospital were good and doctors used them to help combat shock. Donors, including John with his 'O' group blood, had bolstered stocks in the weeks leading up to the Blitz, aware that continued raids and the ensuing injuries would deplete supplies. That night, John held blood bags aloft for patients, first with one arm then the other. Now the hospital was running short, and the use of the blood had to be restricted.

The main storeroom had already been destroyed by a blaze after being hit by incendiaries. It was the same story for the emergency storeroom. Outside, there were more casualties than ever waiting for attention. One was a soldier who had been operating an anti-aircraft gun. Caught in a blast, he had lost one arm at the shoulder, another at the elbow and one leg had been severed half way down the thigh.

Although it was two in the morning, the surgeons went to work on him. By now, the hospital boiler was out of action and a blast had destroyed the operating theatre windows. With no warmth to stabilise patients, they also risked suffering shock. As if to prove the point to the assembled medical staff, the gunner died. Doctors decided to end operations and evacuate the hospital.

More than twenty St John Ambulance Brigade volunteers worked that night, both in the hospitals and in first-aid posts around the city. Some were reduced to breaking up benches to make splints for broken legs. One of their number was killed when a bomb dropped in the grounds of the hospital. 'Whiskers' Harrison was an old soldier who had been in the First World War and bombs meant nothing to him as he organised stretcher parties. In fact, he was some distance from where the bomb fell, but was hit in the stomach by shrapnel.

As a sergeant in the voluntary service, John took a leading role in organising the evacuation. He returned to the ambulance station and rounded up as many men and vehicles as he could. Ambulances waited in orderly fashion for patients to be brought out by stretcher-bearers. In addition to regular ambulances, there were temporary ones, usually made by putting boxes on the back of cars which had had their rear seats removed, following a practice begun in the First World War. Ambulances were maintained by men like John who were often trained engineers.

John saw to it that three patients on stretchers were safely installed in an ambulance, with one placed on the floor, as well as another who could sit upright, along with a nurse and his assistant. But just as he was about to drive away, he heard a shout for help. 'Have you got any room inside?' called a fireman, approaching the ambulance cab. His face was black with smoke and his uniform bore scorch marks. He motioned towards a colleague already on a stretcher and evidently badly hurt. If he did not receive some medical help, the injured fireman was going to die. With some minor adjustments, John thought he could fit the extra stretcher on the shelf that extended along the back of the ambulance. He worked as fast as he could to make his patients as safe as possible before shutting the doors. Then he took the wheel and set off for Warwick Hospital, some ten miles distant. Within moments, he passed an empty ambulance with all its tyres punctured. And soon he could see why. The roads were a mass of craters that had been caused by bomb blasts and, where the surface was intact, it was covered with fragments of blazing buildings, some still glowing with heat.

As the main route was entirely blocked, he negotiated a cautious route along Little Park Street that was shrouded in the smoke which billowed from the ashes of the wooden houses that had previously lined it. Normally, he would have driven with the windows open in case they were shattered by a bomb and thus put the ambulance occupants at risk from flying glass. This time, there were fierce fires to the left and to the right. Without the windows wound up, the heat would have been too hard to bear.

The ambulance made slow progress along the road, and John was uncomfortably aware of the grave danger they and their patients were now facing. The vehicle's fuel tank ran along its side, perilously close to the road. If a spark from one of the numerous fires ignited the petrol, it would mean an explosive end for them all.

Glancing in the rear-view mirror, he saw the cathedral roof alight from end to end. John was once again drenched in sweat. He gripped the steering wheel and headed away from the city centre through a hellish landscape without stopping. He noticed that the anti-aircraft guns seemed to be silent. There was no way of knowing if the operators were dead or if they had run out of ammunition.

It took time and immense patience, but eventually the ambulance found itself out of the line of fire. Driving slightly faster now, John made his way to Warwick Hospital. It was a journey he had made many times before. This time, though, he was surprised to find it in darkness and the staff all in their beds, asleep. Fortunately, he knew where the staff quarters were and, after he woke them, the doctors and nurses were quickly in action. None had any idea before his arrival that there was a major raid going on in nearby Coventry. The hospital was prepared for an influx, though, with emergency beds ready. There were eight wards running off a long covered path for Coventry's wounded. One man – a soldier who had been swinging a searchlight through the night sky to illuminate enemy bombers – had died on the trip, but the rest got the attention they badly needed.

# Chapter Nine

## 'It was as if all hell [had been] let loose that night'

### *An anonymous Coventry Woman*

When it finally came, the All Clear was an understated affair. As the electricity supply had been cut off by the incessant bombing and ARP wardens were still busy away from their posts, just one distant siren sounded. Most people did not move from their shelters or houses until they heard the call of policemen or wardens picking their way through the ravaged streets.

People emerged into the grey daylight, barely able to comprehend that they had survived and with no idea if absent relatives had lived or died. It would be days before some found out. They could not talk without shouting, having been forced to bellow above the sound of the raid all night long. Some were bruised after being tossed from benches and bunks by the force of blasts. Most were cramped from cowering. It would be years before many recovered from the shock.

People had wept, prayed, screamed, clenched their fists, tensed their muscles, shut their eyes and dug their fingernails into the palms of their hands. Everyone had confronted their own mortality as each one of the hundreds of bombs that fell sounded like it was aiming just for them. The night had seemed to last for days rather than hours, but now it was time to take stock, as another cold day dawned. 'The complete silence after the last bomb explosion was as uncanny as the mystery of our survival,' remarked one works fireman.

Apart from physical injury and discomfort, there was a lingering sense of trauma accompanied by a bitter expectation that thousands would be dead. There was little to disavow people of this doomsday prediction as they surveyed the scene. One eighteen-year-old woman came out of the shelter to discover that her family home was gone. She had been warned by a neighbour during the night that this was the case, but she did not believe it until she saw it with her own eyes. The widespread destruction was so disorientating that it was not immediately clear where the building had once stood. All the family's possessions had turned to dust. Her first thought was the dog, locked in a cupboard in the house during raids. But there was no sign of the pet.

The landscape of the city centre amounted to little more than several shaky-looking edifices, a small forest of chimney stacks and piles of smoking rubble, with the occasional twisted iron girder emerging. In the suburbs, shredded blackout curtains fluttered forlornly through shattered windows in road after road. In one roofless house, a bed was balanced precariously on a windowsill. In another, the flames were still eating away at house foundations, while numerous bedrooms and bathrooms were exposed by the blasts, resembling open doll's houses. A sizeable amount of sturdy staircases were still standing, justifying the decision of many to seek shelter beneath them.

As if people were not feeling vulnerable enough, many had the entire contents of their lives exposed to public gaze. Streets were littered with debris, including the shell cases jettisoned by the mobile anti-aircraft guns. They were by turns thick with shattered glass or soft mud thrown up by bomb blasts.

There were 200 craters on roads within a mile of the Council House, which survived the bombing, although most of its windows were shattered. Along the main city thoroughfares, tram rails stood upright or at odd angles – with some found inside a house on an upstairs bed and other sections in a school yard a quarter of a mile from the nearest route. Telegraph poles and streetlights were also crazily contorted. Even kerbstones were dislodged and upright. So powerful was the bomb that struck the main stand at Coventry's City's ground in Highfield Road, which backed onto a row of terraced houses in Mowbray Street, that iron turnstiles were later found more than 541yds away in Gosford Park.

The air was pungent with smoke, from explosions and the oil-drum fires lit on the outskirts of the city in a failed attempt to confuse the Luftwaffe. One family emerged to find a dead horse on the doorstep. It had been blown there from a neighbouring field. A pig hanging in a butcher's shop window filled the air with a tempting aroma, cooked in the heat generated by the waves of bombs. In the streets were stray cats, loose chickens, frightened dogs and the occasional budgerigar.

One woman, who worked at the box makers Thomas Bushills in Little Park Street, was soon on her way across the city that Friday morning to return her niece and nephew to their home at Cheylesmore, still reeling from the previous night's raid:

It was as if all hell [had been] let loose that night. The constant crash of bombs preceded by that terrifying whistle as they came down, fire engine and ambulance bells ringing, folks shouting, screaming and crying, a red glow over all from the flames and the air filled with choking smoke fumes.

The devastation was horrifying. So many familiar landmarks were gone. As we walked down Bishop Street from Radford Road and through Broadgate, there were burning buildings on all sides, and folks digging in the ruins.

I was shocked to see that Bushills had become one of the smoking ruins. We had difficulty getting through to Cheylesmore as there were unexploded bombs which caused diversions.

Dennis Adler emerged from Gulson Road Hospital, having spent the night tending victims, on an errand for the matron. He had been asked to send a telegram to the theatre sister who was on holiday in Ireland, a regular break that she often spent recruiting staff. With money in his pocket and a tin hat on his head, Dennis grabbed his bike and made his way into the city.

What he saw made him gape in disbelief. Proof of the terrible stories he had heard in fragments from patients during the night lay before his startled gaze. The city he had known since boyhood was now a strange, unwelcoming place. It was not long before roads full of rubble made it impossible for him to cycle. He was also stopped by a succession of policemen and soldiers, all of whom questioned him closely about his intentions. He made his way to the main post office, only to find it closed. Then he headed for the other offices where he could send a telegram. They, too, were closed. He returned to Gulson Road to tell those still hard at work with casualties about a city that had been blown up and shut down.

One man, walking under 'the rose-tinted veil which hung darkly over the whole city', saw ARP workers with blackened faces and torn clothes 'looking like drunken men. No one spoke. There was nothing to say.'

People had to find shelter, food, water and warmth – all the basic human necessities – in a landscape stripped of everything that was familiar and comforting.

A woman, who had spent the night in the lavatory with her son, son-in-law, husband and their Irish lodger, admitted in her diary that she nearly gave up hope. The following day, she wrote, 'The town is not there any more. It is so pitiful – people are going from one place to another like lost sheep'.

This was all as Hitler had intended. The aim was to create as much physical and psychological damage as possible while putting a key industrial centre out of action.

There was one man standing in the wreckage of his home who had a particularly tainted taste in his mouth. Two years previously, Henry Tandey, the most decorated soldier of the First World War, had been told he had spared Hitler's life in the last throes of that conflict. With the carnage wrought by the Luftwaffe all around him, Tandey allegedly told a newspaper: 'If only I had known what he would turn out to be. When I saw all the people and women and children he had killed and wounded I was sorry to God I let him go.'

There is no certainty that as a private in the Green Howards Tandey did let Hitler live.

Tandey was without doubt famous for his extraordinary courage, winning a Victoria Cross, a Distinguished Conduct Medal and a Military Medal as well as being mentioned in dispatches for his gallantry. He also freely admitted that he never shot unarmed or injured enemy soldiers.

It was Hitler who linked the two men. At the Berghof, his retreat in Bavaria, he had a painting on his wall of a 1914 battle which depicted Tandey. When Neville Chamberlain went there in 1938 in a failed bid to win peace, he noticed the picture and quizzed Hitler about it. Pointing at Tandey, the Führer told Chamberlain: 'That man came so near to killing me that I thought I should never see Germany again. Providence saved me from such devilish accurate fire as those English boys were aiming at us.'

According to Hitler, Tandey raised his rifle then lowered it again when he realised Hitler was unarmed and dazed, on 28 September 1918. Both men waved respectfully before losing sight of one another.

Later research has put Hitler in a different area of the western front at the end of September. It may well have suited Hitler's ends to embellish his war service by a tale of being reprieved from certain death by a celebrated soldier. For Tandey, the story turned out to be a heavy burden.

It was, of course, impossible for Tandey or anyone else to predict that Hitler would return to Germany to found one of the most infamous political movements of history. Hitler later recognised Tandey in the picture and bought it as a reminder of his personal luck.

One popular account has it that Chamberlain returned to England and telephoned Tandey to tell him. Whether a crisis-ridden Prime Minister had the time to make such a call, or indeed if Tandy, by now a security guard at the Triumph Motor Company, even had a telephone, is open to conjecture.

After trying and failing to re-enlist, Tandey, aged forty-eight, became an ARP warden and so he saw the destruction wrought by Hitler's forces in Coventry at close quarters.

\* \* \*

Christina and Len Stephenson made their way back to Coventry from Fillongley under a pink sky that looked more like a sunset than a dawn. With the heavens above Coventry having been a brilliant red for much of the night, they were expecting the worst. Panic-stricken, Christina made her way home, and was relieved to find her parents and siblings had all survived.

Despite a sleepless night, Mary Heath cycled to work early the following morning to do her twelve-hour day shift at Daimler's shadow factory. The searchlights were no longer functioning and she had only the dim light of her bicycle by which to negotiate craters in the road.

In the immediate aftermath of the raid, she had to help salvage components from the factory. It was the first of many days and nights that she did not take her coat off when she got to work. Although the factory was not destroyed, the section where she worked had no roof. 'We were all wrapped up, with hats and scarves. I don't remember having gloves but no one was bothered about gloves, as long as they were alive.'

It was not just machine operators who had to wrap up after the Blitz. Typists learned to do their daily work in outdoor clothing, too.

In a letter to her sister Marge, Mary Latham told of the immediate consequences of the raid: 'On the Friday morning we were still in the cellar at 8.30 am waiting for the all-clear, and we got that fed up of waiting we all went up to see the sight.

'Then we found out the all-clear had gone at 7.15 am.

'What a surprise it was when we got outside the gate. We were that dumbfounded we couldn't speak.'

Mary's own home and that of her sister Marge had largely escaped damage, but the home of one relative suffered a direct hit. Then Mary took her bicycle, hoping to send a telegraph to her sister to report that the family had survived. After two hours, she gave up trying to find a telegraph office that was open and decided to write a letter instead.

There was a firm expectation that the Luftwaffe would return that Friday night to 'finish the job'. Most people were left agonising about whether to stay or go. Yet, with reports of 417 unexploded bombs and eighteen unexploded land mines, the city remained a dangerous place even in daylight. Mary and her family later set off for relatives in Leamington, first on foot and then getting a lift with a neighbour who passed them on the road.

As well as a lack of electricity, there was no gas or water. To quench the raging thirst of her children, one woman took a bottle of lemonade through the smashed window of a nearby shop, leaving a note promising to pay later. She then gathered their belongings and made a slow and tentative journey out of Coventry to find her husband who was working on the production of bomber aircraft in Lancaster.

Later, it was estimated that between 50,000 and 100,000 people left Coventry in the immediate aftermath of the Blitz and the columns of trudging refugees were a striking sight. The *Daily Mirror* sent a reporter to join the slow-moving and shabby parade under skies that were now darkened with heavy clouds and lingering smoke: 'Every road out of the city which had had a bomb rained on it at the rate of one a minute was filled with the same tragic procession.

'Mothers pushed perambulators filled with household goods, their babies lying on top.

'Fathers carried elder children on their shoulders and bundles of clothing under their arms.'

Coventry resident Dick Webb told the newspaper reporter in no uncertain terms that the Germans had been aiming for people rather than military objectives: 'It is a darned nonsense to say that the Germans made any attempt at direct bombing because as I was walking across the fields a bomb fell 20 yards behind me. It threw me forward. As I got up to run, another came down in front of me.'

In fact, five bombs were dropped around him in the space of 200 yards, the last one causing him a head wound. Later, he saw his home turned to ruins by a bomb and used his bare hands to free his wife and her mother who were inside.

Beryl Ann Leadley's father decided to evacuate his family, after seeing the damage caused to their home and the devastation in the city surrounding it.

'The next day my father went out into the countryside to find temporary lodgings for us. He managed to get us accommodation in Eastern Green with an old lady in a farm house. We stayed there from November over Christmas, until the end of February, then we came back when the roof and windows were repaired.'

Schools were immediately evacuated, but the scheme which was run by the Coventry Education Committee was not popular as parents chose to keep their children with the family. Many people trudged away from the city to nearby towns that became uncomfortably crowded, not realising that rest centres established in Coventry remained largely unused.

But there were plenty who opted to stay in the city, too, including Eileen Bees and her family, who emerged tentatively from their shelter with their ears ringing. They had been located by her father and her sister, who had spent the night hopping from one shelter to the next. But no one had any idea what to do next. They could not return to the shell of their home because the street was sealed off thanks to a delayed action bomb. With the weather bitterly cold, Thomas Weston directed his young family to return to the same shelter, although they had had nothing to eat or drink. In the middle of the afternoon, Thomas Weston left in desperation, tortured by the cold, tired and hungry faces of his family. By the shelter, there was a shop that sold cold meats and he banged on the door, hoping to buy something. When there was no answer, he went round to the back of the shop to find a way inside. Moments later, he beckoned his children out and led them to the private lounge of the shop, putting a tray of faggots that had graced the window in front of them.

They had almost finished when the door was suddenly flung open. The shop owners, a Mr and Mrs Derby, had returned from sleeping out for the night. The woman became hysterical, threatening to ring the police and have them all arrested for looting. Her husband was more circumspect. After swiftly assessing the situation, he soothed his wife and turned to Eileen's father. 'If I'd have been in your shoes, I would have done just the same,' he said. By chance, Eileen met a granddaughter of the shopkeepers after the war and they became lifelong friends.

Although mobile canteens soon became a familiar sight in Coventry, Eileen's father was not alone in being unable to find food that Friday. One man in Coventry for the Mass Observation Project (MOP) also found difficulty in finding a cup of tea, mostly for want of water.

When Eileen and her family tried to return to the shelter after this traumatic episode, they were told that an unexploded land mine nearby had led to its being sealed off as well. After another night spent in a different shelter, the family lived with one son's future in-laws for six weeks until they were rehoused by the council in Binley.

Some people decided to stay, and the sight of people cooking food in a frying pan over the remaining fires – and sharing the ensuing meal with neighbours – became commonplace. One businessman man had a consignment of fresh rabbits that had recently been delivered. He built a fireplace of bricks at the top of his garden and then retrieved the rabbits from his warehouse, fetched an ex-army cooking pot from Coventry scout headquarters in Warwick Road Church and helped his wife to cook a stew to share among neighbours.

Still, according to some accounts, there was very little of the 'Blitz spirit' in evidence in Coventry on that chilly Friday.

Pearl Hyde, the head of the city's Women's Voluntary Service and a future Lord Mayor, was asked by reporters if she wanted reprisals. 'At the moment we jump three feet in the air if anyone slams a door. All we want is a quiet night tonight.'

The same fretful feelings were detected by volunteers for the Mass Observation Project, who were in the city on the day after the raid. Begun in 1937, the MOP was the work of observers and diarists acting as amateur anthropologists, studying 'the science of ourselves'. Anxious to report on the behaviour of people caught up in a concentrated Blitz, the MOP investigators under the leadership of Tom Harrisson, a founder of the project, arrived to find 'an unprecedented dislocation and depression in Coventry' on Friday.

> There were more open signs of hysteria, terror, neurosis observed in one evening than during the whole of the past two months together in all areas. Women were seen to cry, to scream, to tremble all over, to faint in the street, to attack a fireman …

Nearly everybody knew somebody who had been killed or was missing and plenty of people who had been rendered ... homeless ... These subjects occupied literally 90 per cent of all conversation heard throughout Friday afternoon and evening.

Observers defined the dominant feeling on Friday as one of utter helplessness: 'The tremendous impact of the previous night had left people practically speechless in many cases. And it made them feel impotent. There was no role for the civilian. Ordinary people had no idea what they should do.'

As darkness approached the sense of panic and desperation increased. However, that was distinct from defeatism, insisted the MOP witnesses, and there was certainly no threat of civil disobedience. Most people were 'full of admiration' for the wardens in the ARP, the firemen in the AFS and the gunners of the Anti Aircraft Artillery. But provision for defences was largely deemed inadequate.

These were the findings of independent observers written as they happened. In subsequent years, the words of the observers in the MOP have been both supported and derided by people who survived the Blitz. Unsurprisingly, the picture reflected in the *Daily Express* on Saturday 16 November was subtly different. It gave a much more sanitised view of how people were feeling in Coventry, in keeping with government policy: 'They who survived walked with blankets over their heads, bundles under their arms, away from their shattered homes, shaken and shocked, but by no means panicked.

'The wardens said they had no hysterics in the night; no terror, no stampede. People had wept – I saw there were many with red eyes – but they had a courage that kept them sane in the midst of this insanity.'

The scene around the smoking ruins of the cathedral was indicative of this. Men and women had gathered to weep at the loss of an emblematic building that was held in genuine affection and respect in the city. People would talk about the loss of the cathedral and all it had meant to them for years afterwards.

Although one of the cathedral's stonemasons, Jock Forbes, had soon fashioned two charred timbers into the shape of a cross and put them up in the ruins, later associated with the phrase 'Father, forgive', it would take years for that message to resonate among the bomb-battered and bereaved.

An outpouring of high emotion was just what the government had feared, given the singular lack of success Britain had enjoyed during the war so far. (RAF victories over the Luftwaffe during daylight dog-fights in the summer probably seemed hollow to Coventry people that day.) Senior figures suspected there might be riots in Coventry after the ordeal of the bombing. Consequently, soldiers and policemen were dispatched there in numbers to quell any insurrection. By dawn, an extra 200 policemen were already patrolling the streets. A further 600 troops were sent for, with 140 earmarked for traffic control and the remainder for rescue and clearance work.

Perhaps because of the prevailing doubts about Coventry's ability to withstand a substantial blow from the enemy – rooted in the fact that it was a working-class city – the Home Secretary Herbert Morrison was on the scene within hours of the All Clear. He met the mayor and other local officials and his personal fears were presumably calmed because afterwards he paid tribute to the work of the National Service units of the city, who had 'stood up to their duty magnificently'. He told reporters that the Civil Defence volunteers 'displayed great courage and determination under exceptional strain' and presciently declared that the tragedy had only made people more determined on victory.

Nonetheless, Coventry reeled in the morning after an air raid that Germany's official news agency described as 'the most severe in the whole history of the war'. To those pinned down for hours by heavy fire, there was little to indicate that the city had been properly defended. Although there had been some activity by the RAF, it took place miles away from the Midlands.

A squadron from Coastal Command bombed the runways at Vannes and eight Blenheim aircraft dropped thirty-two bombs on the aerodrome in St Leger. Berlin was hit by 17 tons of high explosives, six 1,500-lb land mines and 4,000 incendiaries, with military objectives including power stations. There was a twin attack on an oil refinery at Hamburg, and two aircraft attacked the beam transmitting stations on the Cherbourg peninsula, apparently knocking at least one out of action.

But these mildly successful operations were bracketed by two monumental failures.

The first plank of Operation Cold Water, established in response to Operation Moonlight Sonata and promising to mangle the messages sent by *X-Gerät* transmitters, was a fiasco. There was an uncharacteristic blunder in Britain by those devoted to the scientific sabotage of the German Air Force that permitted the Luftwaffe something of a free rein.

The jammers already established to thwart the operation of *X-Gerät* had to transmit at a particular frequency in order to fool German pilots. On 14 November, the frequency was set wrongly, not by much but it was sufficient that the attempted interference by the British-based jammers was easily audible to Luftwaffe men and consequently quickly disregarded. Thus, the pathfinders of KG-100 were able to fly to Coventry unhindered and off-load the incendiaries that lit up the city for the waves of heavy bombers who came in their wake.

Dr Reginald Jones, who was largely credited with undermining the threat posed by the *Knickebein* and *X-Gerät* innovations, was furious about the error. It was a case of the difficult things being done well, he later explained, but the 'lack of attention to a seemingly trivial detail' caused a slip-up. The person responsible should have been shot, he declared.

His outrage may have been misplaced. Given the sharpness of the moonlight, offering clarity to every contour of the British countryside, it is unlikely that successfully jamming the radio frequencies would have had an appreciable effect on the outcome. Although one geographically significant lake south of Coventry had been drained so it did not act as a signpost, a glance out of the cockpit window was sufficient to show German pilots their position.

Meanwhile the 'concentrated fire' by night fighters as pledged in the final line of Operation Cold Water failed to happen.

There were 121 patrols flown by 123 British aircraft that night, but no decisive interception was made, despite the to-ing and fro-ing of 437 enemy aircraft. Sorties were made by ten Beaufighters which had entered service just two months before, thirty-nine Blenheims, twenty-two Defiants, forty-five Hurricanes, four Gladiators and a single Spitfire. No doubt each was manned by brave men with proven records.

Although Luftwaffe planes were detected eleven times by the fighters – some of which had the latest interception equipment – as well as a sighting by searchlights, only two engagements were made resulting in damage to two

Luftwaffe aircraft at the most. One was downed at Loughborough by anti-aircraft guns.

It was, conceded one report, a disappointing number of combats, a fact that was blamed on the exhaust glow from the Hurricanes 'which has the double disability of interfering with the pilots' vision and acting as a warning beacon to enemy bombers'. Poor vision through the perspex screens of the Blenheims and the Beaufighters, a well known issue that was rectified soon afterwards, was 'a contributory factor'. The first victory by a Beaufighter came on the night of 15 November, when an aircraft from 604 Squadron destroyed a Junkers Ju 88 near Chichester in Sussex.

The large number of aeroplanes caused congestion at radar stations and confusion in the Observer Corps. Meanwhile, the bright moonlight had made single-beam searchlights 'practically useless', according to one report.

For their part, the German aircrews reported seeing seven fighters 'with lights burning' between the coast and the target, without there being an engagement.

Most RAF aeroplanes would have been unable to discern the height at which enemy aircraft were flying, making success in their task improbable. The toll for the night's work by the RAF was ten bombers missing, with two more crashing into the sea and a further one coming to grief on landing. None of this was known in Coventry on the day after the Blitz, bombed as it was into isolation, with communications down and roads leading to it closed.

Firemen were still wrestling with blazes that kept reigniting that day. The aim was to make the city dark by the evening, so that its location might be hidden if the German bombers returned. Their efforts earned the admiration of anti-aircraft gunner Donald Lee.

After breakfast, he had gone to bed and slept soundly until the bugle sounded for the one o'clock meal. He was due to begin seven days' leave and was going to make his way home to Birmingham. But he found there was no transport and as he made his way on foot to the city centre, he was horrified to see areas of 'utter desolation'.

Rows of houses [were] demolished, tremendous craters here and there, with hastily rigged signs marked 'detour', some to the left, others to the right.

As I neared the centre of the city the smouldering of the buildings was still going on. There would be occasional bursts of flame and the firemen were still playing their hoses [on them] and this had been going on ever since the raid started. The men must have been out on their feet.

One tally revealed that 121 shops were destroyed, 131 more were badly damaged and 432 were continuing to trade. The strength of the fire in some shops had been so severe that silver coins in their cash boxes had melted.

In a bid to raise morale among shopkeepers, the Ministry of Information issued white posters with two Union Jacks in the corners and a blank space in the middle for them to scribble any piece of personal abuse they wanted to direct at Hitler.

About 1,000 houses were wrecked beyond repair and a further 30,000 suffered bomb damage. Five churches, six theatres, including the Scala and the Gaumont, and the Central Library were razed. Ten hotels and public houses were also flattened.

Despite the gloom that inevitably pervaded the city, the view of the city's officials was more upbeat than that of the

MOP. According to the Chief Constable, Captain S.A. Hector, 'After the raid ... the people were shaken but when they found they were being taken in hand and looked after they soon came round to helping each other a bit, although later in the day several thousand made private arrangements to evacuate.

'At present the temperament of all is undoubtedly that of determination to see the war through until Hitler is beaten.'

As early as 10.40 a.m. on the day following the raid, he was able to report to Whitehall that the situation was 'now in hand'. In a telephone message to the Home Office, he said that the number of casualties was likely to be severe but that the numbers could not be accurately estimated because of the breakdown in telephone communications and the difficulties that messengers were encountering on the roads.

'In hand' was perhaps a sufficiently vague term to embrace what was going on the city. The substantial number of people who had become refugees in fear of another raid would at least not be pressing for food and shelter. That made the task of the Emergency Committee considerably easier. While those who stayed were not on the verge of rioting, they were being scarred by the kind of sights that inevitably followed such a large-scale bombing raid.

Two men carrying a stretcher with a blanket-covered body on it were pursued down the street by a little girl screaming 'mother'. Another two children, who were sisters, waved when they recognised each other across a hospital ward – unaware that the rest of their family had perished. Body parts littered the city centre – on high wires, amid rubble and on the clothes of the living who had escaped death by inches – and they continued to emerge for weeks afterwards. For the unwary traveller around the city after the raid, there were severed limbs, headless bodies and disembodied heads waiting to be discovered. Stretchers covered with blankets that were being taken from bombed sites often looked curiously flat because rescuers were often only able to retrieve a proportion of a dead body, as the rest was missing.

Factory worker and Red Cross volunteer Dilwyn Evans helped to pull people out of the rubble as part of a team of four that had been allocated sites by the police. He had spent the night at Armstrong Siddeley tending to minor injuries after cycling there from his home through the bombing raid. Now, his first priority was to stem any sense of rising panic by talking calmly to those who were trapped. He also prevented well-meaning passers-by from intervening. 'There were always people willing to help you but in a lot of instances people did harm rather than good.'

It was a painstaking job. Each piece of debris had to be removed by hand, a physically exhausting task for the rescuers who were constantly re-evaluating their approach so they did not cause further injury. According to Mr Evans, people pinned down in the wreckage were often prepared to lie back and wait for liberation. He helped to free more than twenty people.

Even when people were dead, he and his colleagues approached the task with care and consideration. 'We had a feeling of reverence. I thought to myself, "I'm not going to hurt the body any more", even though the body couldn't feel anything.'

Mr Evans was no stranger to grisly sights; he had witnessed two people walking into the giant rotating propellers in the aero engines test department of the factory. Still, pulling bodies from the rubble was demoralising work, and he admitted it was frequent cups of tea offered by field kitchens and WVS vans that kept him going.

Later, Pearl Hyde reflected on the service done by her band of women and others during that difficult time: 'You know you feel such a fool standing there in a crater holding a mug of tea ... until a man says "it washed the blood and dust out of my mouth" and you know you have really have done something useful.'

Ultimately, Coventry people did not starve in those straitened times. Army field kitchens and mobile canteens were established as soon as possible in the streets. Food was salvaged and sold – although a lot of tinned food could not be saved having 'popped' in the heat. Bread and milk vans from neighbouring towns then arrived for roadside trading when it became clear Coventry bakers could not safely produce bread.

Other undamaged cafés opened up to distribute free meals. For two weeks, rationing was suspended to ease the difficulties facing families who opted to stay in the city. The manager of Woolworth's café in Coventry was loaned to the Emergency Committee as an organiser to help with the supply of hot meals. While fresh and frozen meat was taken to Birmingham in the absence of a refrigeration system in Coventry, some 60,000lb of canned meat was rapidly dispatched to the city.

And it was not long before radical improvements were made. A contingent from the Royal Corps of Signals arrived to establish a temporary communications system within the city. Eight miles of piping were brought in to set up a water supply to standpipes. It was not just water pipes large and small that had been damaged – mostly in a two-mile radius – but also five pumping stations, which were paralysed by a lack of electricity. However, the post-Blitz water supply was not clean, and a message to boil water before using it was broadcast around the city by loudspeaker vans to avoid an outbreak of typhoid fever. Nor could people use toilets; they were urged to dig a hole in the garden to use for calls of nature. Residents were also urged to seek inoculation and three centres were soon opened to give protective jabs.

About 300 gas mains were fractured and there was extensive damage at the gas works where a gas holder was completely destroyed, along with the engineering offices and the main stores. Miraculously, there was no damage to the 33,000-volt main transmission cables that distributed the electricity supply to four primary substations. However, two primary substations and seven secondary ones were rendered useless.

St John Ambulance Brigade volunteer Dennis Adler continued working at the Gulson Road Hospital. Before the day after the raid was finished, Dennis, who had been unable to send a telegram at the behest of the matron, went aboard one of the single-decker buses that were used to transport patients ten at a time to Barnsley Hall Hospital in Bromsgove.

The buses skirted Birmingham where a raid was underway, and when he arrived in Bromsgrove, he was given a meal, a bath and a bed for the night.

He discovered one of the patients ferried there from Coventry was his uncle and another was a young girl who lived in the same road as he did. He left the following morning, promising to contact their relatives, who almost certainly feared that they were missing or even dead.

Only hours after the German raid ended, the Midland Red Bus Company presented a fleet of vehicles at Coventry and Warwickshire Hospital, too, with all the seats removed. So the evacuation of the hospital's injured continued. People were transferred to other nearby hospitals or, if they were well enough after being patched up, to their homes. Of course, they could not return alone. Many found their houses damaged or even that they had disappeared. John Sargent worked as part of a team of stretcher bearers, mostly transporting the injured from hospital bay to bus.

The task took them all day. In Leamington, he had found time to send a telegram to his brother Gilbert, who was serving in the Army. It was not until 6.00 p.m. that he and his partner Doug finally found their work was at an end. They had eaten little more than Horlicks tablets all day. When they finally realised they were hungry, they headed for the hospital kitchen.

Often the pair had dropped by the kitchen during duties at the hospital to find a friendly cook who would rustle them up some food. Now it was deserted. The windows were blown in and the pair had to pick their way carefully to the larder.

In it, they found bread and cheese swathed in grainy brick dust. They did not look appetising, but after only the smallest hesitation, the pair brushed off the dust and ate the food. John and Doug returned to the ambulance station to find it badly damaged by a series of bomb strikes. But one room filled with stretchers was still standing and appeared solid enough.

They discussed the possibility of the German bombers returning. Both knew the water supply was patchy and that the anti-aircraft guns lay unmanned. But, as both men had been awake and working full pelt for thirty-six hours, they decided they probably would not even hear enemy aircraft that night if they came. After washing their faces and hands, Doug and John found an empty stretcher and settled into a deep sleep.

Len had to stay at the Coventry Climax factory until 11.00 a.m. the morning after the Blitz to give bosses a tour of the devastation that had been caused. Everyone agreed the clear-up process would not start until Monday.

Factory workers such as Len were paid one shilling and six pence an hour to clear up the wreckage – a lot less than the wage they were used to as skilled labourers – but no one complained. The most important job at hand was to salvage whatever was possible from the factory in the shortest time and get it back into production. For now, though, he had a three-day break before he was due back at work.

He went to his girlfriend Cecilia's home in Earlsdon, to discover that the factory where she worked, Bushills in Little Park Street, had been burned down. She had already visited a second Coventry Climax site in the city, only to be told that the one at Widdrington Road had been destroyed. When Len and Cecilia saw each other for the first time in the wake of the raid, both burst into tears of relief. Her home had survived, all bar a back window frame that was dislodged.

Above all, they wanted a good night's sleep. With the prospect of the German bombers returning, Len decided to evacuate for the forthcoming night at least. He agreed to meet Cecilia again at 4.00 p.m.. He headed back to the house where he had lodgings, hauling his bicycle over piles of rubble and gazing for a few moments at a land mine dangling beneath a tree whose branches had snared its parachute. It was swaying gently some 10 feet above the ground.

When he finally reached his home in Moat Avenue, he saw the damage caused by a land mine that had exploded. Six houses were destroyed. The house where he lived had its windows blown out. He noticed small shards of glass glistening in the wall and ceiling where they had become embedded. The front door and the roof were also badly damaged. And there were more tears, this time from his landlady who had been convinced that he had been killed.

When Len met up with Cecilia again, they drove to Northampton by motorbike, and were stopped at numerous police road blocks as they left the city. Each time, they had to produce their identification cards and give an explanation of where they were going. They headed for a hotel where they discovered other civil defence personnel, mostly from London, also seeking some peace. There, they went to the cinema, hoping to distract themselves from thoughts of their battered home city.

The lights in the picture house dimmed, then the siren sounded and a warning flashed on the screen. Len and Cecilia gripped each other's arms, bracing themselves for a shower of bombs. To their surprise, no one moved.

Later the siren sounded again – and once more no one in the audience moved a muscle, except for Cecilia and Len whose bodies stiffened with tension. By the time the air raid warning was heard for a third time, Cecilia and Len had forgotten entirely what the film was about. Their sole concern was to get to a place of safety. But if they shuffled along the row of seats in the cinema, they risked infuriating everyone else in the audience. So, they stayed put, rigid with anxiety. When they finally got to their hotel that night, they slept deeply.

# Chapter Ten

## 'A city of the dead'

*An anonymous Coventry Woman
in a letter to her daughter*

When John Sargent emerged from the ambulance station on Saturday, he found debris piled high outside. The building had suffered three direct hits and six of the Brigade's nine ambulances were out of action. But it was the 800-lb unexploded bomb lodged on the driveway in front of the hospital that was causing the most immediate difficulties.

John's sleep the previous night had been unbroken. Although 310 enemy planes were recorded in the skies over Britain on the Friday night, they had stayed away from Coventry, choosing targets in London and other parts of the Midlands instead. There was also a serious attack on Bournemouth. John felt ready to tackle some of the immense problems that lay before him.

Together with other volunteers, John decided it would be possible and even prudent to move the inert bomb. There were obvious dangers in dealing with explosives like this, which now pock-marked Coventry. It was possible that some were faulty and would never explode, since German munitions were made by forced labour who contributed in any small way they could to the downfall of the Reich. More likely, the bombs had a hidden timer that delayed detonation,

176

so it was impossible to tell at what point they would explode. Accordingly, streets were cordoned off, but ambulance men, among others, simply removed the barriers and carried on through if they were on their way to collect casualties.

John had already encountered a policeman from Birmingham who had been drafted in to help keep law and order in the days following the Blitz. He told John how he was looking down at an unexploded bomb wedged in a crater that it had made when he felt the ground beneath his feet begin to move. Because he was a young man, his reactions were lightning fast and he turned to sprint away as quickly as he could. Although he was blown off his feet, he escaped the worst effects of the bomb as it exploded.

However, the bomb at the ambulance station was preventing every effort to get it back in working order. Having survived the Blitz all the Civil Defence volunteers such as John were clear about one thing, they would rather die quickly, above ground, than endure a slow death trapped in an air raid shelter or similar. So, five men collected together as many crowbars and pick axes as they could muster and began heaving the bomb from its resting place. Their none-too-gentle operation came to a sudden end when an Army Bomb Disposal truck screeched to a halt nearby.

A sergeant emerged from the vehicle using sufficient swear words to make the ambulance men blush. In essence, he wanted them to step away from the bomb. As they meekly obeyed his orders, they spotted one of their own sergeants sheltering behind the stout brick wall of a nearby building, clutching the first aid kit. Bashfully, he stepped into view and admitted he was waiting there to help if the bomb had gone off. They had been subdued by the army officer, but now they fell around laughing. 'As if the plasters and bandages in the kit would have helped if the bomb had gone off,' said John later. 'We'd all have been in bits.'

John saw for himself just what damage a bomb blast could do later the same morning when he and Doug were called to collect the body of a man who had been blown right over a three-storey building when an explosive ignited. With every bone broken, the victim's body was like jelly. It was impossible for John and Doug to manipulate the corpse onto a stretcher. In the end, they found a piece of tarpaulin and rolled the man's body onto it so that they could transport it to the mortuary. There were other deaths too caused by unexploded bombs in Coventry. Three salvage workers and one employee were killed at Humber Hillman, where components for Rolls-Royce engines were made, when a delayed-action bomb concealed by debris exploded fifty hours after being dropped.

With the city still counting its dead, the atmosphere remained mournful and downbeat despite the non-appearance of enemy bombers on Friday night. A much-needed boost to morale came in the shape of King George VI, who made a surprise visit to Coventry on Saturday in a visit arranged at less than twelve hours' notice.

Dilwyn Evans was at work in his capacity as a Red Cross volunteer in the wreckage of the High Street, trying to recover a dead body, when he felt a tap on the shoulder. It was the Coventry Mayor Jack Moseley, who had only been in the role for five days before the raid, who quickly introduced the King.

'[The King] put his hand out and thanked me very much for what I was doing,' said Mr Evans. 'That repaid me for everything I had done.'

'I was surprised because no way did I think someone like that would be there. When I stood up and saw him there … it was more or less like a dream, like a mirage.'

Mr Evans was awarded an MBE in the 1941 New Year's honours list.

Resplendent in his Field Marshal's uniform, the King also encountered a man carrying two chickens that he had rescued from a crushed coop. Before he left one man called out, 'Good luck your Majesty. Stick to it. We're ruined but we're happy'.

Then the royal visitor made one last home visit, to the Moseley household. According to family members, Jack's wife Nell was sweeping up broken glass in their home when the royal party arrived. Not realising who was knocking, she called to them to go around the back – and found the King entering her kitchen. As for Jack, he had spent Friday touring the city in the company of the King and was unshaven and without a collar and tie when the monarch arrived to say an unscheduled good-bye.

One newspaper highlighted the significance of the royal appearance.

'Today the King came to this stricken industrial centre for a first hand view of the destruction wrought by the Nazi bombers and personal contact with some of the victims of Göring's villainy.

'Coventry was not slow to understand and appreciate this practical demonstration of His Majesty's sympathy.'

Comparatively few people encountered the King in the same manner as Mr Evans and the saviour of the chickens. Most heard about the visit via newspapers and newsreels. But, as planned, the visit succeeded in raising the spirits.

Infected by the significance of the occasion, the editorial in the *Daily Mirror* two days later read:

The royal visit to Coventry and other places afflicted by the foul enemy touches the British public deeply.

The King goes as the sovereign head, not only of a great and free people, but as the first representative of civilisation fighting against the German pestilence.

In his courage, gentle personality and practical knowledge of affairs, King George symbolises the democratic ideal at its best.

Dilwyn Evans was one of many rescue workers who confronted grisly scenes as they tried to clear the city of its mark of death. Another, Jenkyn Shanklyn, worked tirelessly in the aftermath of the raid, and released one woman from the wreckage of her home. But that was not the sum total of his achievement. In the following week, taking little rest or food, Shanklyn collected eighteen mutilated bodies from Barracks Square at the Old Rover works and then a further twenty-two scorched bodies from in and around a collapsed hotel in Jordan Well. His tireless devotion to an unsavoury but highly necessary task earned him the British Empire Medal.

On the day of the King's visit, a Minister of Home Security inspector also came to Coventry to make a report: 'At a very rough estimate, one third of the factories in the city have been either completely demolished or so damaged as to be out of commission for some months,' he wrote. 'One third have sustained considerable damage which will hinder production for some weeks and about one third have been only slightly damaged. A few escaped altogether.'

Already on the Saturday, there were signs that the people of Coventry would endure their lot with resilience. One observer from the Mass Observation Project related his experience as he tried to secure breakfast:

All one could get for breakfast was biscuits and cheese and milk in a little shop-cum-refreshment room. The elderly shopkeeper remarked to another patron in between serving him and someone else that her husband was 'under that lot' – meaning the wreckage of a nearby surface shelter which had suffered a direct hit and under which lay many dead bodies. She introduced this information quite casually without any apparent emotion and then went on with her work – which consisted to a great extent of telling people that she hadn't any bread.'

Mary Latham returned to Coventry on Saturday, trying to comprehend as best she could what had happened. With roadblocks in place to stop anyone entering the city, she had hidden under blankets in the back of the car being driven by her uncle on his way to work as a chef in a local factory. 'I stood and cried, it was awful to see it,' she told her sister.

There isn't a shop left from the Geisha Cafe to Harvey's in the Burges, even Owen Owen has gone.

West Orchard and the old market and all Smithford Street is demolished, everywhere is a mess.

I was in the town when the King was there, but I didn't see him.

Eventually I started back to Leamington at 4 o'clock and I landed in Auntie Bele's at 7 o'clock; all that while to get there, but it was worth it to have a good night's sleep.

By Saturday, a squad from the Royal Navy had been set up in Coventry to defuse unexploded landmines. Sub Lieutenant

John Miller, who led the team, described the problems that they found when they arrived on Friday afternoon: 'Our eyes smarted and ran in the heavy smoke. It was clear that there was going to be grave difficulty in the mere finding of our mines. Most streets were blocked with craters or fallen buildings ... the telephone system was out of action and it was obvious that communications both within Coventry itself and with the outside world would be next to impracticable.'

Nonetheless, based at ARP offices in Leamington, he successfully got a list of the mines that had been reported thus far and a map of Coventry in order to prepare for the job in hand. It proved trickier to find beds for the night for the team, with all accommodation on the outskirts of the city taken up by refugees. 'Had it not been for the strong line taken by the Admiralty and the Ministry of Home Security it would have been impossible,' he wrote later.

A hotel was eventually persuaded to help and secured billets for officers 'in the houses of well-to-do residents in the town'. Unfortunately, the ratings who were there to assist in defusing the mines were taken to a grandstand on Warwick race course by soldiers charged with finding them accommodation, where they were told to sleep on wire mattresses beneath a single blanket. With no blackout curtains at the windows, the men were unable to strike a match so that they could see to hang their hammocks. Finally, they chose to sleep in a neighbouring room on a concrete floor.

There was no dinner for them on the Friday night and, although breakfast was provided the following morning, there were no utensils and the men had to eat with their fingers.

'We made such a row about this that the next night and for the rest of the time the men were accommodated in billets similar to our own,' said Sub Lieutenant Miller, who clearly suspected the long-standing rivalry between the services was at least in part to blame.

On Saturday, the team had fifteen mines to deal with, but found Royal Engineers in the process of blowing up the more dangerous of them after cordoning off the city centre. As Miller said, 'We forced our way through the cordon, our drivers, incidentally, showing considerable courage.'

Almost immediately after getting to work, two of the Navy men hit problems when a mine was accidentally detonated. After shouting a warning, the bomb disposal expert gathered his tools and ran to an underground shelter some 50 yards away. The sailor accompanying him initially ran in the wrong direction, but was at a similar distance when the mine exploded and he escaped with shock and a few grazes.

By Monday, the threat of land mines had been dealt with, but the team stayed until Tuesday in case any more were uncovered. By the time they left, they had been impressed by the conduct of Coventry people – although they wrongly believed that more than half the city's police had been killed during the raid.

'We were very much struck by the behaviour of the civil population in the city,' wrote Sub Lieutenant Miller, who was later awarded a George Cross for his work in bomb disposal. 'Apart from other difficulties there was a shortage of food but, though there was scarcely a policeman to be seen on the streets (and many of what there were were strangers who had been hastily drafted in from Worcestershire and other places) the people behaved with perfect coolness and order which was a great help to those who were trying to assist them.'

By now there was a perceptible desire among residents to stay in Coventry with the return visit by the Luftwaffe now seeming less of a threat. On Sunday morning, about 300 people turned up to be evacuated, following calls issued by the city's emergency authority. Arrangements had been made for 10,000.

The Mayor remained hard at work, trying to lift the spirits of those most affected by the raid. He visited Coventry evacuees in a Leamington school, one of twenty-one centres outside the city, as far flung as Worcestershire, Warwickshire, Leicestershire and Northamptonshire. With the influx of refugees, Leamington experienced a water shortage and the borough engineer urged residents to economise. But a letter written by a Coventry woman to her daughter on the Sunday reveals that there were still abundant concerns among the city's bewildered population. In the letter, she described Coventry as 'a city of the dead' with no bread or milk supplies: 'I have not seen a house that has escaped. We are among the lucky ones as we only have our windows smashed and part of the roof bashed in.'

She and her husband had sheltered in the 'cubby hole' for eleven hours and there was, she said, no lull in the bombing.

Our knees trembled. We seemed to sit and wait for death as we heard roofs crashing and glass flying ...

There is nothing left of Broadgate. The cathedral is in ruins, only the spire left and that doesn't look safe.

The central library has gone, the market hall has gone. In fact I think it would be easier to say what hasn't gone. The centre of the town is roped off, no one allowed within half a mile of it ... they are talking about blasting the town because none of the buildings seem safe.

Mrs G has just told me that one can't get near the Council House for people waiting for death certificates …

I have never seen so many soldiers. The town is full of them, clearing the debris. The military powers have taken over the city and everyone has to obey orders.

There were improvements, even if they were imperceptible to the dazed general population, who were by now seizing upon a sense of pride, having survived the worst ever bombing raid. By Sunday, only four fires still smouldered in Cox Street, Whitefriars Street, Jenner Street and Bishop Street and the glare was deemed insufficient to attract the attentions of enemy aircraft.

However, publicity surrounding the raid was causing a bit of a stir.

For reasons of security, the detail of the enemy bombing raids remained unclear in newspapers, radio and film reports so as not to confirm or deny Luftwaffe success rates. Charged with walking a fine line, the BBC had already been criticised for its 'bland' offerings that were little more than transparent propaganda. For the first time in November 1940, the BBC named Coventry as a city targeted by the Nazi hierarchy and flattened by enemy bombs. The BBC was not the only news source to identify Coventry, either. British Pathé News, which was seen at cinemas, described it as 'the martyred city', with the commentator declaring 'the courage of Coventry is an example to the whole world'. But, by using emotive language and stating the numbers of casualties, the national broadcaster attracted criticism from the War Cabinet – which then had high-level discussions about denying the BBC independence and bringing it firmly under government control.

At a War Cabinet meeting held on Monday, 18 November, Herbert Morrison, the Minister of Home Security, admitted that the casualty figures had been issued in his absence. But there was, he insisted, an advantage in stating the number rather than have rumours and exaggerations pass into common currency. Alfred Duff Cooper, the Minister of Information, pointed out that publicity had improved the morale in Coventry. Obviously a source for the BBC, he said he had prohibited any reference to the fact that the attack was concentrated on the centre of the city, which was why a number of factories were not badly damaged.

Even Churchill was in favour of the BBC's reportage. The effect 'had been considerable' in both the United States and Germany. The prominence given to Coventry came at a time when Britain was trying to shape American public opinion towards war. Given that there were many towns in the United States called Coventry, its miserable fate seemed to strike a chord. Churchill himself doubted the degree of publicity given to the raid on Coventry had done any harm, although he was concerned that information was now only given to the press at ministerial level. However, Anthony Eden said he had listened to a special account of the effects of the air raid transmitted by the BBC on the Saturday night. It was, he said, a most depressing broadcast, which would have had a deplorable effect on Warwickshire units.

The War Cabinet asked the Chancellor of the Exchequer Sir Howard Kingsley Wood, Herbert Morrison and Alfred Duff Cooper to investigate what changes, if any, were necessary in the constitution and management of the BBC in order to ensure its effective control by the government. It was the moment that the BBC could have been reeled in from its independent state to become a mouthpiece for the state.

The War Cabinet already had considerable influence over the content of daily newspapers, with Lord Beaverbrook – the owner of the *Daily Express* among other newspapers – a government minister responsible for aircraft production. Ultimately, the ministers realised the value of having news that was not overtly doctored as it was in totalitarian states and the BBC was permitted to continue unfettered.

Germany responded to the BBC's news broadcast by announcing apparently truthfully that 223 of its citizens had died in the raid on Hamburg carried out on Friday 14 November. Perhaps the authenticity of the BBC broadcasts chimed with German news announcers, who were usually famously awry with the truth.

A documentary by the Crown Film Unit, called *Heart of Britain,* soon captured the widespread destruction for broadcast. But there was a different view broadcast on the propaganda radio station Workers' Challenge, which purported to be run by a group of socialists in Britain when, in fact, it had been created by Josef Goebbels earlier that year.

Coventry is the first place to be attacked in this way outside of London and Liverpool but we are bloody sure it's not going to be the last …

Most people thought it wouldn't be too easy to smash up one of the biggest production bases in the country but it was done …

It is impossible to describe what happened in Coventry … the BBC says that military objectives were not hit. That is just bloody bunk and everybody knows it. All attempts to hush the thing up broke down because from the industrial point of view there is none of Coventry left.

There's never been such a bombardment before, either in this country or anywhere else in the world relative, that is, to the size of the town. All night long the bombs fell without pause. The place could be seen for miles. Loss of life is appalling. Nobody knows how many casualties there were because there were so many bodies under the ruins. But one thing is certain: every single death that occurred must be laid at Churchill's door.

The broadcast, which was monitored in Britain, went on to criticise the government for keeping men at work when they should have been in deep shelters. And it was Goebbels who then glibly coined the phrase 'Coventriat', a new verb referencing the raid, meaning to destroy. Everyone seemed to want to paraphrase the physical and emotional state of Coventry and its people with just a few words.

In fact, Coventry was neither a 'city of courage' nor completely down and out. The truth lay somewhere between the two, although there was a darker side to the aftermath that was barely broadcast afterwards.

Shops were getting back to business. Unnecessary signs often warned customers of the retailer's predicament. One typical hand-drawn board read: 'Shopping will be chilly but you will receive a warm welcome'. Still, looting – the blight of all similar urban catastrophes – emerged as a problem. According to the police, it had not been a feature of previous raids in Coventry. But there were eighty-seven cases following the Blitz, with at least thirty-six cases reaching court. Among those charged were three soldiers, three auxiliary firemen, four youths and two girls.

It was not primarily personal possessions that were pillaged, but rather cash and the pre-paid meters, common in houses where there was a 'pay-as-you-go' system for electricity and gas supplies. During 1940, the police were told of 800 meter break-ins and also 456 cases of bicycle theft. Oddly, one twenty-eight-year-old man was sentenced to three month's hard labour for stealing an eighteenth-century register from the city's cathedral. Three firemen got six months in jail for pilfering from a shop.

A letter written in 1946 to Coventry's town clerk indicates that the practice was probably widespread, but did have consequences for at least one looter.

With the letter came a collection of coins taken from an Oxo tin found buried in the fruit and vegetable market by a soldier who had worked in the city in 1941 on demolition and clearance: 'I realise now how indifferent I was to the suffering and loss of your city of Coventry when I was there amongst the ruins of buildings,' the writer admitted. 'To search for buried goods was of more concern to us than the keeping of fatherless children and the deep mourning of a stricken city. I realise in myself how far short I came to what I should be.' The letter was signed 'a repentant sinner'.

Coventry was not alone in suffering crime during its darkest hour. Nationally, a staggering 10,000 people were prosecuted for looting. Traders in London believed that more of their goods were looted than were destroyed by bomb damage.

Rationing was also widely abused, perhaps because everyone suspected fellow citizens were on the make. Abandoning rationing in Coventry after the Blitz to help feed the starving was a major concession by the authorities and it caused a great deal of envy elsewhere.

Most of the notable wartime crimes happened outside Coventry. For example, on one occasion in Britain, five million clothing coupons were stolen, leading the government to cancel the entire issue. By 1945, there had been 114,000 prosecutions for black-market activities. Among that number was the popular entertainer Ivor Novello, who was given eight weeks in jail in 1944 after accepting stolen petrol coupons from a female fan.

The smartest criminals even donned the uniforms of ARP wardens while they unloaded goods from shops into which they had often smashed their way. Sometimes, on seeing the ARP insignia, unsuspecting onlookers would help to load the getaway vehicle with loot.

In June 1941, the *Daily Mirror* reflected on the 'smears and blots' that gave lie to the notion of a Blitz spirit in Britain: 'How else can be described the profiteers, the pilferers, the black market bosses, the tobacco twisters and all the crafty little crooks of the make-a-bit-extra brigade? These people must be rooted out, suppressed and punished.'

Bystanders to the event were also guilty of unseemly behaviour as people began to be pests. In another unsavoury aspect of wartime behaviour, hordes attempted to visit the city after its fate was announced, treating it as some unusual daytime entertainment and diverting resources from where they were most needed. At least one policeman threatened to prosecute sightseers for misuse of petrol. The patience of busy policemen was already being tried by time-wasters taking advantage of the newly installed replacement telephone line. 'The police have been embarrassed by the extraordinary number of unnecessary phone calls made by people inquiring as to damaged property,' said an outraged *Midland Daily Telegraph* on Monday 18 November. 'With only one telephone line in operation these calls are preventing essential work proceeding.'

# Chapter Eleven

# 'Our men without exception behaved like heroes'

*St John Ambulance Brigade report*

At the top of Coventry's Emergency Committee's priorities was the need to provide people with a square meal washed down by copious amounts of tea. The WVS served 50,000 meals in the three days after the raid. Within a week, there were seventy canteens in action distributing free food to approx 20,000 people a day, with another sixteen kitchens attached to rest centres.

Even those people whose houses were not bombed were experiencing problems putting a meal on the table. For many, Friday was pay day and the disruption of the Blitz meant that a large number of people were left without the pay packets they relied on to feed their families. In some cases, employees had approached their works on the day after the Blitz demanding every penny that they were owed so they could leave the area. But many workers no longer had jobs because their factories had been bombed.

With an increase in unemployment, there was 'emergency relief' available at the local employment exchanges. At one stage, 15,500 Coventry people were signed up for this.

Hope was fading for those trapped under rubble. But there were celebrations when, four nights after the raid, a squad of rescue workers pulled a woman out alive from the debris that had once been her home. She had been sheltering under the stairs with the rest of her family during the raid and she was the only one to survive.

Shovel-wielding soldiers had made huge progress on clearing roads so that vehicles – including tractors and other clearance machinery – had access to the city once again. Ferrying shattered bricks and mortar out of the city was a massive task and painfully slow to complete. Most of it was dumped in the surrounding fields. Some of the debris was deposited in a crypt of the cathedral, where it lay undisturbed for almost seventy-five years.

By the end of Sunday, the railway system was operating again, except for the stretch between Coventry and Nuneaton. The restoration of services represented a huge achievement by railway workers as one three-and-a-half-mile stretch of track had been hit forty-two times and the damage included a 60-foot-wide crater. On the Monday night, the fire brigade was called to seven outbreaks of fire at old incidents, none of them serious.

The following day, a medical officer turned up at the ambulance station to ask for volunteers to put dead bodies in coffins so that they could be buried together in a mass grave. Without hesitation, John and Doug stepped forward. The prospect of dead bodies held no fear for them.

They made their way to the makeshift mortuary that had been set up in the gasworks. At the beginning of the war, the gasworks was cleared of coal stocks as it was an easy target from the air. Now, a building next to it was being used to store the bodies of those who had died in the hail of ordnance. No refrigeration was necessary – the weather was so cold that, even during the day, the temperature lent itself to the storage of the dead.

The building used as a mortuary was lined with racks and runners that would take an ambulance stretcher and which were several layers deep, the upper layers being uncomfortably high to load. Bodies wore luggage labels revealing where each had been found, their identification, if it was known, and the number of the ambulance which had taken the body to the mortuary, all written in lead pencil. All bodies had to be identified before a death certificate could be issued.

Unfortunately, the makeshift mortuary now lacked its corrugated iron roof, thanks to enemy action. Within a few days, pouring rain soaked the bodies and washed the writing off the labels. One of the hazards of blast injuries was that identification became difficult or impossible. Sometimes, people were identified by the clothes they were in or the belongings that they carried.

At the door of the mortuary, John stopped for a moment and wrinkled his nose. The smell of burnt corpses lingered in the air. The army officer in charge had a workman-like approach and soon had volunteers on the move as he shouted 'Don't stand on ceremony'.

Occasionally, they would break off if a funeral director came in to collect the body of a victim if his or her family sought a private funeral. But that soon ended as the Emergency Committee decided on mass civic funerals, which upset some people who had already not been allowed to view the bodies of the dead. The decision did make some sense: coffins were in short supply and the paperwork involved in arranging private funerals was onerous.

It was heavy, sombre work. When a soup kitchen arrived, workers like John looked at their filthy hands. There was no water in which to wash or any soap that would kill the germs. One man said, 'I couldn't eat a thing after everything we've seen today.' John stared at him for a moment, then shrugged and said, 'Well, I'm not going to die with an empty stomach.' Drinking straight from the bowl, he consumed the vegetable soup at speed.

By Monday, three days after the Blitz, 380 bodies had been recovered and removed to mortuaries. The revised figures of wounded was now reported as 800. There were thirty-eight outstanding incidents to be cleared where it was believed that bodies still needed to be recovered. People crowded around the Council House where lists of the dead were compiled, looking for names of relatives and friends.

The city was dogged with rumours about the fate of the missing – specifically, whether large numbers of bodies had been sealed in collapsed shelters by the authorities. This was partly fuelled by the smell of rotting flesh that pervaded the area around Broadgate in the days after the raid. Indeed, a lack of water meant that the entire city smelled rather unsavoury. The cause was discovered to be some putrid meat in a wrecked cold store. There was even talk of people being kept alive underground by secretive authorities who, for reasons unknown, would rather disguise what was really going on.

Eventually the *Midland Daily Telegraph* made a public announcement in an attempt to end the speculation: 'In the last few days it has been widely stated that not only are many bodies still buried beneath piles of debris and that in some cases central shelters are being sealed up but that a number of people trapped on the night of 14 November are still alive and being fed regularly by tubes. Such statements are authoritatively declared to be incorrect.'

With uncertainty remaining over how many people had died and who they were, it was hardly surprising that people were susceptible to wild stories. The confusion was such that one fourteen-year-old girl,who had been evacuated from Coventry and Warwickshire Hospital to Stratford-upon-Avon, saw her own name on the mortuary list outside the Council House.

There were other rumours too: that a man caught signalling with a night light had been shot; that a Luftwaffe plane made a vapour trail in the shape of a swastika or a tick before the raid to warn fifth columnists to leave the city; that the cathedral's tower had been spared to act as a beacon for future attacks, and that 400 employees at the Standard enamel shop were buried by a direct hit. These were the collective fruits of embattled imaginations.

There was no undeclared pile of corpses in any of the city's factories. But, although staff had come from Birmingham Register Office to speed up the system, there was still an achingly long queue of bodies to process. By Tuesday, 19 November, the infants were moved out of Whoberley school, which had escaped virtually unscathed, so that 200 gravediggers could be accommodated there.

That Tuesday, Dennis Adler's status at Gulson Road Hospital changed. He had been working every waking hour to assist in the crisis. He even slept at the hospital while his parents and younger brother moved to the outskirts of the city. But five intense days at work took its toll. Dennis collapsed with pneumonia and changed from helper to patient. He had kaolin poultices applied to his chest and was given one of the early antibiotics commonly called M&B 693.

Dennis was sent away to convalesce and, by the time he returned home, the Christmas decorations were already in place.

The first civic funeral took place on Wednesday, 20 November, at a time when bodies were still being recovered. The first 172 victims were laid to rest in four long, narrow trenches at the London Road cemetery after the coffins arrived under tarpaulins on the backs of trucks. Aircraft patrolled overhead to ensure that the service was not disrupted by enemy action. Black-clad mourners, many with injuries, heard prayers from clergymen in surplices, with steel helmets and gum boots. The service was led by Dr Mervyn Haigh, the Bishop of Coventry, although all faiths were represented.

In his address, the Bishop told the people that the eyes of the world were upon them and that their spirits should remain unbroken: 'I wish I could show you some of the hundreds of letters I am receiving from all over the country asking me to express to you admiration and trust. We must not disappoint those hopes and we shall not ...

'In this city we have been better friends and neighbours than we have ever been before.'

In the wintry sunshine, the people of Coventry filed passed the trenches in which the coffins had been placed head to toe. The edges of the trenches were transformed into a sea of flowers as people laid anything from single blooms to mighty wreaths.

A further 250 people were buried the following Saturday. Alas, the funerals did not put an end of the suffering for Coventry. There was a further tragedy for sixteen Coventry citizens who believed they had found sanctuary in nearby Kenilworth after the Blitz. A raid that hit the small town on 21 November flattened a coffee shop and a pub, killing at least twenty-four people, the majority of them the refugees from Coventry.

For those who sought spiritual comfort but had seen their churches destroyed, altars were established in two Coventry hotels: the Grapes Hotel and the Pilot Hotel.

\* \* \*

By 23 November, 3,415 schoolchildren had been evacuated. A letter dated that day from a Coventry woman to her daughter, reassured her there was plenty of food but admitted that life was far from normal:

> Soldiers are everywhere, standing at the end of streets with fixed bayonets, asking you your business. Furniture vans are constantly moving people's homes. People seem to think Coventry isn't a safe place to live anymore but where is there a safe place?
>
> Kenilworth is packed with Coventry people and the other night they dropped a land mine in the centre of it.
>
> We did have one quiet night, the night after the raid. But every night since we have had [German aircraft] over and many times during the day.

There were many worse off than herself, she conceded.

And at last there were some signs of a recovery and of the 'Blitz spirit' that had been at times conspicuously absent reemerging among the population.

Before joining the Army, Bill Wilson, a future Labour MP for Coventry South and South East, ran into an acquaintance, Fred Brigden, a First World War veteran. Fred asked nothing more of life than to dig his garden, watch the Bantams play – as Coventry City were then called – and listen to the wireless. Bill recalled, 'I saw Fred the Sunday after the Blitz and naturally asked "How are you?". Fred told me: "I have been down the factory. We haven't much of a roof but we are starting work tomorrow. We'll beat this bugger yet."'

And there were some heart-warming stories emerging from the chaos. Len and Christina Stephens decided to get married almost immediately after the air raid, fearing that each day could be their last. Before going to the service, Len stood in the remains of the cathedral looking up at the point of the 300-foot spire. For the first time, it seemed it was crooked and he wondered if it had somehow been warped by the fire. He had heard how witnesses saw the building blocks of the cathedral glowing with heat from numerous fires. The smell of its destruction was still hanging heavy in the air, as continually low-lying cloud had acted like a blanket.

Reaching into his breast pocket, Len felt for two small, square black boxes. He flipped open the lids to reveal a pair of shiny, gold wedding rings and held them aloft, for a silent blessing.

For the wedding at the end of November, Christina wore a dark blue suit that she had bought for work. She weighed up the chances of buying or making a wedding dress but life was so topsy-turvy after the Blitz that she knew trying to find one would be a wasted effort. When she looked around at the wedding party, with Len's mother in a black coat and her dad in a navy three-piece, it struck her that they seemed a mournful-looking group. A bombing raid the previous night had once again left everybody shaken.

It was not helped by the fact that the city was covered in a thick fog. It had been hardly possible to see a hand in front of her face when Christina had left her home for the register office.

Inside the atmosphere was equally sombre. Electricity supplies had still not been restored, so the room was lit by two candles on the registrar's desk. There was no photographer in attendance, as it was impossible to buy reels of film. A baker managed to provide a horseshoe cake suitable for the occasion. It had been ordered before the Blitz, but was not collected on the appointed day. Clearly, the bride who had initially chosen the design was among the Luftwaffe's victims or had decided to cancel plans because of the raid. Home for Len and Christina was now an end of terrace in Forfield Road, solidly built just before the war, with a stone bay window.

The Blitz and its aftermath also led to the marriage of Len and Cecilia Dacombe. Len was called into Coventry Climax and told that the factory was re-locating to Oswestry, in Shropshire. The company was relying on Len to establish the new factory and train local workers. He asked for time to ponder the decision, deciding immediately that he wanted to go with Cecilia by his side. Unfortunately, Cecilia's father was disabled, so her income had been vital to her family's finances. But with the destruction of Bushills, she now worked only at a first aid post, earning much less than she had previously and the family had to adapt accordingly. The couple finally married on 8 February 1941, living first in Coventry and then in Oswestry.

Both Len and Christina's and Len and Cecilia's marriages lasted more than seventy years.

Many tributes were paid to the people of Coventry and what they had endured. A report about the St John Ambulance Brigade recognised the work carried out by John Sargent, Doug Henderson, Dennis Adler and others:

> It was when the bombs actually fell on the various wards that our men without exception behaved like heroes because it will be appreciated that there was no light in the wards and although not very full, they had to be emptied.

It was the reliability, calmness and courage of our people with the assistance of some of the hospital staff that enabled all patients without exception to be moved to places of safety ...

Some of our men went into buildings in a state of collapse and rescued people but it was all in the night's work and all on duty worked with a courage that had to be witnessed to be realised ...

No one relaxed their energy on the transport side but worked under indescribable conditions with great fortitude. Men who had lost their vehicles and could do no more joined rescue squads and continued helping wherever possible.

Factory bosses also lined up to deliver words of sterling support to their workers, albeit from some distance. Samuel Courtauld, the industrialist and art collector, sent his message to textile workers on the pages of the factory newspaper *The Rayoneer*: '[My] sympathy goes out to those employees who have lost relatives or perhaps their homes and belongings. We are all proud to know that Coventry has taken this blow with its chin up. Such courage in a week during which there were many examples of heroism on land and sea and in the air calls forth the admiration of the whole world and leaves no doubt as to the ultimate issue of this struggle.'

Workers would receive a New Year's gift of five shillings for those aged under eighteen and ten shillings for adults, he announced.

In the New Year's edition of the *Alfred Herbert News* a message from Albert Herbert himself underlined the spirit that finally prevailed:

A brutal aggressor thinks that by the indiscriminate bombing of women and children he can break your morale. You have given him an answer, he is biting on granite.

In this war we are all in the firing line, fighting for everything which makes life worth living. Everyone, by doing his appointed work to the best of his ability, is taking his share of the load.

There is a long and bitter struggle ahead. Do not be deceived by any apparent slackening in the enemy's attack, he is only preparing for fresh and more determined efforts.

For a brief spell, Coventry remained at the heart of the news agenda. But as the Luftwaffe turned its attentions to Birmingham, Liverpool and Southampton within weeks the Blitz in Coventry was superceded by new tales of horror and heartbreak. Abroad, there were looming difficulties in North Africa and Greece. Soon at least some parts of the government began to move on from the crisis in Coventry.

If the British government was keen to move on from the Coventry raid, the Germans were happy to dwell on it for a while, still insisting that they had dealt a heavy blow in an attack that started immense fires of raw materials, which were visible as far away as the Channel coast. On 2 December, an English-language broadcast from Germany said a Spanish journalist had described the town as looking 'completely disrupted, as if by an earthquake'. A week later, the first pictures of Coventry and Birmingham following their respective raids appeared in the German press.

\* \* \*

After the November raid, the directors of Rover agreed to pay £100 to the dependants of the two firemen who had died on their premises. In addition, they offered sums of £500 to be paid at the discretion of the managing director to those who had lost loved ones and property. Other funds included the Alfred Herbert Air Raid Distress Fund.

Generous donations from across the world were also made in the name of the suffering at Coventry. In December, the Mayor announced: 'We are receiving clothes and money from all parts of the world ranging from a cheque for £5,000 to 6d from little children in the north.'

A cheque for £215 was sent by the people of Hucknall in Nottinghamshire. 'It is a drop in the ocean of your requirements,' the accompanying letter said. 'The people of Hucknall, many of whom are descended from Warwickshire miners and pit sinkers that came to the Leen Valley coalfield 60 to 70 years ago, have been deeply shocked by your calamity and greatly moved by your fortitude. The money subscribed has come very largely from the humblest among us.'

The general public were not the only ones to respond. Evelyn 'Boo' Laye, one of the most popular artistes of the era, visited the Hippodrome on Saturday 7 December to mark its re-opening. The celebrated soprano received a bunch of flowers from her second husband, Frank Lawton, because it was their anniversary, and she auctioned them off, selling each bloom for a pound, to help raise money for the city.

Laye was a personal friend of King George VI, and was much admired by him before he met his wife. Indeed, it was Laye who introduced him to the Australian voice coach Lionel Logue who eventually helped cure the King of his stammer.

Supporting her was the comedian Stainless Stephen and the musical comedy duo Mr Flotsam and Mr Jetsam.

Although it was the first time they had worked since the Blitz, the stage-hands, orchestra member, call boys and cleaners gave their services for free that night, while AFS men and ARP wardens were offered cheap rates of entry.

Everyone agreed that it was vital for Coventry and her industry to be up and running as soon as possible. But such was the need elsewhere for men – as well as machines – that there were soon rumblings about substantially reducing the number of troops clearing Coventry amid a feeling in London that the presence of soldiers was the 'easy option' and reduced the incentive to use civilian labour. The number of soldiers in the city at the time amounted to one field company of Royal Engineers, one engineering construction company, two Home Defence Companies of the Pioneer Corps, one works company of Royal Engineers and 900 infantry soldiers.

A letter from Anthony Eden, the Secretary of State for War, to the Minister of Home Herbert Morrison, dated 5 December 1940, said that the soldiers involved were due to head for the Middle East and that helping in Coventry was seriously interfering with their training. He asked that the unemployed be mobilised so that the troops could be released within a few days. The following day a tartly worded response was sent from the Ministry of Home Security: 'In the first place I can assure you that very active steps have been taken to recruit civilian labour to assist in the work of restoring industrial production and repairing the local services and I cannot understand the suggestion in the letter that nothing is being done.

'It is possible that Western Command have not fully appreciated the limited nature of the local labour reserves.'

Not every unemployed person in Coventry was suited to the work of clearance and repair, the letter said: 'Moreover, as vital factories are restarted men who might be available for emergency repair work are withdrawn. Local unemployed men have been taken on but it is also necessary to recruit men in large number from outside the area and this is being done at a rapid rate.'

Importing any form of labour brought its own problems in terms of finding the necessary billets and transport. It was not a case of mean-minded householders refusing to let rooms. In any case, the government had compulsory powers but was still unable to find sufficient beds:

> You will appreciate that the repair of houses must proceed at the same time as the repair of factories in order that workmen may return to the town ...
>
> The withdrawal of the troops within the next 24 hours would have a very serious effect indeed upon the restoration of essential war production in Coventry and I am sure [Herbert Morrison] would wish to press most strongly for an extension for the period of stay of the military until civilian labour is fully available in the district.

It felt like a triumph that rooms for some 700 people had already been found, of which 550 were filled. Beyond that, a camp was organised on the city outskirts to house 2,000 more workmen. There, workers would be safe from raids and so would benefit from a good night's sleep. Still, the authorities were not likely to obtain any other accommodation until houses were habitable again.

People were prepared to suffer enormous hardships, given the circumstances. During the raid, an incendiary had welded itself to the bath in one home and for years the owners bathed with the incendiary bomb until the bath was finally replaced. But in the cold winter weather, windows and roofs were considered a bare minimum.

Cabinet ministers, including Eden and Morrison, were united in believing that soldiers and civilians were working well together. On the ground, it was not always the case. In the immediate aftermath of the Blitz, army lorries had stood idly by when public transport for displaced workers was sorely needed.

Hugh Beaver, the Controller of Building Material at the Ministry of Works, was concerned that both civil authorities and junior officers were not pulling together to get the best out of the men who answered to them. 'Many of the soldiers are putting in only two or three hours work a day and, in view of the seriousness of the position in Coventry, more effective control is needed,' he said.

An engineer by trade himself, Beaver – who was knighted in 1943 – recommended that a consultant engineer should be brought in to supervise when cities were Blitzed.

It was not the only criticism of what had occurred in Coventry. The equipment issued to rescue parties who came to the city to help after the Blitz was found to be inadequate. In particular, the absence of light, mobile cranes was noted. One regional Civil Defence paper said: 'Lack of technical direction generally has hindered progress considerably, many [rescue] party leaders not having any idea as to how to tackle a difficult job.

'It is suggested that rescue parties might be composed of five skilled men with a pool of labourers available to be drafted to the site of a serious incident where they would work under the five skilled men of the party.'

Rescue-party leaders and the men in their charge had little or no elementary training in the dangers of gas, water and electricity mains damage. And incompatible equipment that hampered collaboration between the local authority fire brigade and the auxiliary fire brigades from factories also came in for censure. Within months, the National Fire Service had been formed, amalgamating 1,400 fire brigades nationwide and ensuring that there was standard equipment on hand.

As the New Year dawned, the housing crisis continued in Coventry. By then, there were 3,071 men doing 'first aid' repairs to homes, although at least 600 additional men were urgently needed. The shopping list for skilled tradesmen went like this: 200 carpenters, 50 plasterers and 50 plasterers mates, 50 bricklayers and 50 bricklayers mates and 50 plumbers, with a similar number of helpers. Carpenters were at the top of the list for without them, the slaters were held up.

Fourteen thousand houses awaited repairs and even though some 20,000 homes had already been made habitable, many of those still needed further work. Families squeezed in together where they could. Betty Daniel's Uncle Arthur and Aunt Kezia moved in with family members after their house was wrecked. They had been sitting either side of the fireplace when an incendiary crashed through the ceiling and landed between them and were lucky to escape without serious injury.

Perhaps typically of the era, the bureaucracy surrounding the clearance and repair of Coventry was mind-boggling: insured goods in small shops were dealt with by the Board of Trade, while food stocks came under the remit of the Ministry of Food. Bricks were the responsibility of the Office of Works, while timber and steel fell under the aegis of the Ministry of Supplies. And disused materials were the responsibility of the local authority but it fell to the public health authority to deal with putrefied material. Soon after the raid one Coventry resident complained: 'The authorities are making the most of the raid ... they see themselves as martyrs with a job that will last for the duration.'

# Chapter Twelve

# 'Surely another war will destroy civilisation'

*Mary Bloomfield*

Gradually a sense of normality returned to Coventry. More people returned to their homes after gangs of workers made wrecked houses habitable. Slowly, standpipes disappeared from street corners as clean fresh water began running once more from domestic taps. Shortly before Christmas, electricity and gas supplies finally came on line again. Perhaps of greater national significance was the fact that factories were soon back in production, grinding out new aeroplanes, military motor vehicles and a whole variety of guns, ammunition and assorted supplies.

But when Coventry was fully back in harness for the war effort the Luftwaffe decided to return, although not in such great numbers as in November.

On 8 April 1941, in the week leading up to Easter, there was another heavy raid on the city that lasted nearly seven hours. Some 230 Luftwaffe bombers were involved, dumping some 315 tons of explosive and a further 25,000 incendiaries on the city. The death toll was 281. Two nights later, the enemy aeroplanes came back. The raid was shorter and sharper, but still claimed the lives of a further 170 people. Those who lived on the outskirts of the city were most at risk this time, as the Luftwaffe avoided the flattened centre and aimed for the suburbs.

This time, the Coventry and Warwickshire Hospital was one of the main casualties, despite the large, red cross on its roof that was intended to denote its humanitarian nature and save it from attack. It suffered ten direct hits, devastating the infrastructure and killing patients, nurses, doctors and three stretcher-bearers. A hospital sister, nurse and a patient were killed when a bomb hit the X-ray Department, but most of the casualties were claimed by a delayed action bomb that burrowed unnoticed into the building and exploded at 7.00 a.m., after the All Clear had been sounded. Twenty-one patients who had been sheltering in the basement lost their lives alongside doctors and several nurses. All the hospital's windows were shattered and there was no heat or water as a result of the bombing. The building was left in ruins.

There were some incredible tales of courage shown by hospital workers. Mary Beardshall from Stoke was operating the switchboard that night, although her usual job was as porter. When a bomb blast blew the walls in on top of her, she suffered a fractured skull but managed to escape from the debris. Regardless of her injuries, the twenty-eight-year-old mother of four used her hands to smother incendiaries before holding up a collapsing beam to allow other people to get safely out of the wreckage. Her bravery won her a George Medal, but curiously, she vanished after leaving her children with their grandparents when she joined the ATS the following year.

Matron Joyce Burton and nurse Emma Horne helped to free trapped victims, offering practical help and medical assistance, and both won George Medals.

The hospital's destruction added to the confusion that inevitably followed any large raid, as casualties were shipped out of the area. Those left behind did not know if the injured were alive or dead.

This was the era before the National Health Service and hospitals funded themselves by a variety of rudimentary insurance schemes. In Coventry, supporters donated a penny a week, to what was known as the Saturday Fund to ensure that the hospital stayed operational. After the April raids, the Saturday Fund, which had been operating since 1870 and was based in Swanswell Terrace, sent a message to donors through the columns of the local newspaper urging them to continue paying: 'Our buildings are down but our service is at its peak. Please post contributions as normal. It is difficult to send out as we are real [sic] busy. Callers should come to the rear of the premises – we shall welcome them.'

Once again the toll on families was immense. Marjorie Edge, whose family escaped virtually unscathed in the November Blitz, except for the loss of a flock of chickens, was by now eleven. Weary of the cold and damp nights spent in the Anderson shelter, her mother had for some time opted instead to stay under the stairs at the sound of the siren. The heavy raid on 8 April left them petrified, but their spirits soared when, during a lull in the bombing, they heard the familiar, chirping whistle of their father William who had returned from the Daimler works – where he was seconded from Courtaulds – to see how the family was faring. With relief, they monitored the comforting sounds of the routine they knew he would follow. They heard the click of the gate as he went to garden shed to deposit his bicycle. They heard the door latch open before he stepped into the house. Then suddenly their straining ears were filled with a rushing, howling sound followed by an explosion and the repeated thud of cascading bricks.

Once the air was still again, Marjorie's mother Annie pushed the understairs cupboard door open and told her younger children very firmly to stay put. After a while a torch illuminated Marjorie's anxious face and she was told to follow the man who held it, without touching anything. She noticed there was no ceiling or roof so she could see straight into the night sky. Then she spotted her father being laid on to a door that was perched between the settee and the sideboard. There was no sign of blood and Marjorie assumed that he had been knocked out by the rubble. Marjorie, her brother Raymond and her younger sister Eileen went to stay with neighbours while her mother and older sister Vera tried to locate William after he had been taken to hospital.

With the extensive damage done to the city hospital, William had been transferred to Nuneaton, where he died two days later without regaining consciousness. He had probably dived under the table when he heard the bomb falling, but the tumbling masonry broke his neck. Peeping out of a neighbour's window, Marjorie saw her mother walk home from the bus stop on the day he died and knew by the expression on her face what had happened.

Annie refused to have William buried in the communal grave that by now housed hundreds of the city's dead. Instead, he was laid to rest with her mother in St Paul's churchyard, to be joined by her father, Marjorie's grandfather, the following year after he died of cancer.

After William's death, Annie was told by the hospital staff that her husband would have been mentally and physically disabled if he had lived. She heard, too, from Daimler workers that the shelter that her husband would have used had he stayed at the factory was also hit by a bomb. But the effects on the family were nevertheless devastating.

The benevolent society attached to Daimler offered some financial resources to them and the children were all kitted out with new clothes that had been sent to Coventry by an American Christian society. Church hall tables were laid out and covered with these donated clothes. For the first time, Marjorie heard the term 'sweater' and developed a huge attachment to her own new purple one. Momentarily, it distracted her from what would now be a disjointed childhood with a widowed mother and a bombed-out home.

On the same night, perhaps in the same string of bombs, the St John Ambulance's headquarters nearby took a direct hit.

Eileen Bees and her family had been enjoying living in the spacious and luxurious home assigned to them by the council in Binley. But it offered no greater protection in the April raids than had their previous home. After a crack appeared in the wall of their new house when a neighbouring house took a direct hit, the family moved to the nearby schoolteacher's home, which remained untouched. Soon after the bombs had stopped, Eileen's youngest sister Amelia, aged three, started vomiting. It was almost impossible to summon medical help, given that telephone lines were once again destroyed, but the popular consensus was that shock was the cause. However, the sickness continued and it became marked with blood. Amelia had her fourth birthday on 11 April and died three days later in her mother's arms. A post mortem discovered that the cause was a burst lung, which she had suffered during the raid – even though the rest of the family had suffered no ill effects. Sadly, the family's torment was not over as, on the same day that Amelia died, thirteen-year-old Olive and seven-year-old David were admitted to an isolation hospital suffering from diphtheria. Fortunately both survived.

Alan Hartley's twenty-eight-year-old neighbour, Kenneth Johnson, was among those killed at the Coventry and

Warwickshire Hospital. A conscientious objector, Johnson worked at the Coventry Gauge and Tool Company by day and as an ARP stretcher bearer at night. After the raid on 8 April, Alan's sister Joyce was evacuated to Barrow-in-Furness to live with their father Harold, not knowing that just weeks later the Luftwaffe would inflict devastating damage on the town. Bombing raids against Barrow were carried out on 14 and 16 April and for a week starting on 3 May. The primary target was, of course, the shipyards. However, the railway station suffered a direct hit and a crane used by two fire watchers was brought down, killing both. Before the Luftwaffe were finished, the attacks on Barrow had killed eighty-three people and more than 300 people were injured, partly for want of public shelters, and some 600 houses were wrecked.

Back in Coventry, two sisters Ethel and Janet Loveitt, aged fifty-eight and sixty-two respectively, both died on duty as Civil Defence wardens at Grosvenor Road during the second of the April raids. They were the spinster daughters of Coventry's chemist Thomas Loveitt. Another woman, who had been widowed in the November Blitz, died trying to shield the body of an elderly and bedridden friend.

John Sargent's home in Humber Avenue lost its roof. He thought he was about to lose his life after seeing a string of bombs head toward him and Doug while they were fire watching from a rooftop. Fortunately, the final bomb dropped just short of the building they were on and they sped downstairs to help casualties in a nearby shelter.

Dennis Adler had by now recovered from pneumonia. Advised against doing physical work, he got a job at the Food Office, reissuing ration books that had been lost or destroyed, but he still spent his nights at Gulson Road Hospital.

During the Easter Blitz, he saw an incendiary drop into the laundry building and quickly alerted the hospital's senior medical officer. Together, they smashed a window and tackled the blaze, extinguishing it before it caused extensive damage. Only afterwards did they discover that the door to the laundry building had been open all the time.

A third mass funeral was held at the London Road cemetery after what is commonly known in Coventry as 'the forgotten Blitz' because most of the national and international attention in subsequent decades was directed firmly on the attack in November, given that it was the first concentrated attack of its kind, despite the heavy loss of life experienced later.

Thankfully, the damage to the city's infrastructure was not as catastrophic as it had been previously. Most people had access to a water supply almost immediately, although once again the water had to be boiled. The prospects of those affected getting a decent meal were also better. Once more, the fleet of WVS food wagons rolled into action, this time with the benefit of experience. Cookery teachers were withdrawn from schools to help in emergency feeding centres. A baker in the town gave away racks of hot cross buns that he was unable to sell because his shop had been wrecked.

Other lessons had been learned, too, thanks to the November raid. A report by the chief fire officer had pointed out that blackout material in shops should be removed at night-time because they hid the flames of a fire sparked by an incendiary until it had firmly taken hold. Sprinkler systems in buildings had not worked well because aerial bombardment brought down the very ceilings they were installed in. However, the presence of water reservoirs in factories across the city did, although few new ones had been built in the intervening months for the matter of cost.

Before the November Blitz, fire brigade stores had been kept at three different locations in Coventry, all of which were bombed. Now the stores were spread more thinly and widely. Rescue parties were reorganised after November when one report found that 'a lack of technical direction generally ... hindered progress considerably'. In essence, while they were good for shovelling rubble, many rescue party leaders had no idea how to tackle jobs that involved gas, water or electricity supplies.

Once again firemen – most of them part-timers with full-time factory jobs – leapt to the defence of the city. When the last blaze was extinguished, the thoughts of many in the city turned to the widows and orphans who remained following the deaths of men in the fire services. Three station officers and six city fire fighters had died as well as a number of men in the auxiliary service and people chose to express their gratitude by digging deep into their pockets. The September 1941 annual report of the Coventry and District Associated Fire Brigades recorded a total of £868 9 s 1 d in the welfare fund, more than six times the figure for the previous year. That included £175 10 s raised at Armstrong Siddeley and a personal gift of £50 from Alfred Herbert. The total was announced a month after the local authority and auxiliary fire services amalgamated to become the National Fire Service, at a time when the association comprised fifty-two brigades. A year later, the widows and orphans fund stood at a magnificent £1,394 11 s 9 d.

But money could not replace those who had died, nor could it replicate the city that had been lost. Those who lived and worked in Coventry had to get used to a life lived among ruins. Although they were soon cleared of rubble, roads remained closed as the repairs were carried out to underground pipes. Prefabricated buildings started popping up where once individually impressive architecture had stood. Drab, half-cylinder Nissen huts now dotted the landscape while some bombsite basements had been cleared and converted into water storage tanks to fight future fires. In many parts of the city, the water mains now ran above the ground, disappearing below ground only at road junctions.

One of the most pressing needs remained that of accommodation, not least for the increasing number of women workers who came from inside and outside the city. In 1939, the number of female employees in the motor vehicle, bicycle and aircraft industries in the city was a modest 3,800. Within two years, this had increased to 13,900. This figure rose still further as the war continued, and does not take into consideration the many who were working in munitions and other factories.

In Coventry, the National Service Hostels Corporation made rooms available around the city. They were in utilitarian buildings, designed to be simple and cheap to put up. The women shared basic dormitories and were provided with meals, which were eaten in a communal dining room. Recreational activities were sometimes organised, and some hostels had games rooms where the women could relax.

Alongside hostels, there were many Coventry people who welcomed workers into their homes as lodgers. An article in the *Midlands Daily Telegraph* from November 1941 reports that 'no fewer than 16,000 voluntary billets have been found in raid-devastated Coventry'.

Although home comforts were improving for factory workers there was no respite from the grinding schedule at work.

The factories of Coventry faced a monumental task. From June 1941, Coventry workers not only made armaments and equipment for the British war effort, but also for the Russians. Hitler's vaulting ambition was finally revealed in Operation Barbarossa, his surprise attack on the USSR. Now, it was clear that the failed plans to invade Britain were little more than a sideshow in the grand scheme drawn up for the Third Reich. Items made in Coventry went not only to troops in North Africa and to depots across the British Empire but also on convoys across the icy Arctic Sea to Murmansk. With the Luftwaffe now concentrating on the newly opened eastern front, there was less action in the skies over Britain.

The industrial profile of the city nevertheless changed. After November's raid, the government and major industries began to site key factories in different locations, spreading them across the United Kingdom so that they would no longer be at risk of being paralysed by a heavy air attack. Families that were already shattered by homelessness, grief, trauma and the absence of men in the services were further fractured when major companies decided to re-locate.

Even families that remained together in Coventry faced daily difficulties. Newly-wed Christina Stephenson was struggling to put tasty meals on the table and, when a painful lump on her eyelid appeared, one of the local shopkeepers declared the stye was a sign that she was eating too much sugar. If only too much sugar was to blame for the affliction, she thought. Like everyone else, she was subject to rationing and her intake of sugar had been severely curtailed.

Not just sugar but also tea, margarine, butter and all meat were restricted to just a few ounces per person. Altogether, the weekly allowance of food per person would have fit into less than half a shoebox. Christina did not really mind that the contents of her shopping basket were so limited. After all, everybody was being treated the same. But to be accused of having too much sugar was grating. And the antics of the enemy brought a different degree of difficulty to shopping on at least one occasion. One day, as she headed to the Co-op store on the corner of Forfield Road, where her rationing book and those of husband Len were registered, Christina had to lie flat quickly when a single German aircraft firing a machine gun came overhead. Christina still experienced stark reminders of the November Blitz. Shortly after she had married, her uncle cut down a neighbour who was attempting to hang himself after losing his entire family in the raid. Plus, she regularly saw another man leading a small pony down the street, a living link to the child he had lost on that night. Not long afterwards, she and Len moved to Leek in Staffordshire where Daimler relocated to sidestep the effects of any future attacks.

Low-grade tensions simmered across the city in the years after the raids and relationships between workers, bosses and the government gradually revealed fractures. Factory hands were suspicious of the industrialists whom they felt could help increase output through better management. One union convenor accused Coventry engineering employers of actually impeding the war effort and called for a government inquiry into the issue: 'There are numerous American machine tools of the most expensive type which are not yet assembled, although they were delivered some time ago. They stand as monuments of inefficiency in this factory, or glittering untouched jewels.'

Coventry shop stewards went to London to tell MPs about 'slackness and window dressing' in the factories there, claiming that output was '50 per cent' below its possible maximum and that between 2,000 and 3,000 skilled men had been dismissed through redundancy, only to be replaced by women on lower wages. Night shifts were staged only for the benefit of visitors, they said.

The left-leaning *Daily Worker* clearly believed that bosses were prone to picking fights with a workforce despite the national emergency: 'Working to low quotas and not employing plant to its uttermost capacity is the thing to fight against, not high wages.'

For their part, the bosses eyed the overt fraternal feelings between Coventry workers and those in Soviet Russia with grave suspicion, fearing an outbreak of communism.

Admittedly, the entry of Russia into the war had given some Coventry workers something of a political thrill. For just as the bosses dreaded communism, so some of the workers reviled capitalism and sought its overthrow. The wording of this works committee bulletin is typical among activists at the time: 'Our great ally the Soviet Union is bearing at the moment the full brunt of the military struggle. Their losses in material and in life are heavy and grievous. They are fighting and dying for a cause that is ours. They are fighting an enemy that is also our enemy. Utmost production must be our goal.'

Perhaps perversely, Coventry workers and the British government with Winston Churchill at its head were singing from the same song sheet, the Prime Minister having promised Stalin maximum effort. But no amount of enthusiasm for the war effort at home or that in Soviet Russia could keep hard-pressed Coventry workers – not known for being subordinate – passive for long. Tensions boiled over for one set of workers when they heard that government employees were better paid than they were.

The sheet metal workers, earning between £9 and £11 a week, held a sit-down strike for two-and-a-half days after their request for a fifty-per-cent wage rise was turned down. After that, they spent five days away from the factory. All ninety-three men involved were fined £25 when they appeared in court in May 1943. In their defence, solicitor John Varley said that the men were suffering frayed nerves having been working sixty-eight-and-a-half hours a week in a permanently blacked-out factory and having to endure long trips to and from work.

Relentless round-the-clock rotas inevitably affected the health of many and the toll on Coventry's factory workers as the war continued caused anxiety, with the spread of tuberculosis, also known as consumption, a particular concern. In September 1943, the mayor, who by then was Mrs E. Smith, spoke out on the issue at a meeting in London: 'I know the war must be won quickly but I do not like to see our people so worn and pale, working in factories eleven hours a day and doing other work afterwards. I fear for them and I fear for consumption.'

According to Mary Bloomfield's diary, there was more unrest on the home front from September 1944 when factories began scaling back their operations as victory seemed assured: 'Coventry aircraft factories are to receive a 25 per cent cut in personnel. There is bickering between the skilled men and the "dilutees" as to who should be the first to be stopped.

'They say that married women will be the first. Already one hears rumours that such and such a place have sacked many. Some have been told not to start back again after the September break.'

Fire watching had been stopped, and the blackout in Coventry was relaxed from Sunday, 17 September.

Relations between the government and the industrialists who ran the shadow factories were also strained for much of the war. Economies became necessary at Whitehall when it became obvious that the conflict would be a long one and the government sought to reduce the management fees and production bonuses it had initially been prepared to pay for armaments manufacture. For example, in 1941, the government refused to pay more than £41,000 per annum to Rover, whose board had been hoping for the £60,000 that it had previously received. The reduction followed a disagreement about the price of Cheetah X engines. Rover had demanded £1,305 for each one produced, while the government was prepared to pay only £1,000.

As a company, Rover was not facing a financial squeeze. Profits for the year ending August 1941 stood at £97,540 with the highest-paid director receiving £2,500 a year.

Coventry workers were also well paid, and most were voluntarily paying 3d per week from their wages to a servicemen's welfare fund. Yet minutes of the Rover's factory directors' meeting following the November Blitz revealed that the board turned down appeals for subscriptions from army service units in Coventry to help the very men who were defending the factories. A pattern of fundamental mistrust between Coventry workers and factory owners was forming which would endure long after the conflict had ended.

The final air raid on Coventry was a harmless incendiary attack on 3 August 1942. In a two-year period, 1,252 people had died in forty-one raids. Nearly 4,000 homes had been destroyed and almost 55,000 badly damaged. A further 4,500 people were slowly rebuilding their lives after receiving serious injuries.

In 1944, the death toll of the November Blitz was finally announced by the Official Censor. The final figures, it said, were 554 dead and 865 people seriously injured. There have been perpetual rumours that the death toll was actually much higher and some of the reasons why people think that are rooted in logic. Forensic searches for bodies that were destroyed by the conflagration were not possible in the aftermath. Given the honey-pot nature of Coventry, with its opportunities for employment, it is thought there might also have been victims with no immediate family or friends who were simply not missed. Others refused to believe that so few had died in such a large air raid.

One woman recalled the remainder of the conflict with something like affection. A munitions worker, she remembered food queues in which people laughed and chatted. She knitted socks for soldiers and sent letter to sailors on HMS *Coventry*, a veteran of numerous sea battles until being sunk off Tobruk, in North Africa, on 14 September 1942. The woman also raised money to take out invalid soldiers convalescing in nearby hospitals to the theatre or cinema.

There has been some perceptible resentment directed towards Coventry from other regions of Britain that also came under heavy fire during the Second World War, given the attention Coventry garnered for its suffering.

There are many different ways to measure the suffering of those who were attacked by air during the Second World War. The following is as enlightening as any.

According to an official history of Civil Defence produced by the government after the war, London was the worst hit city between 7 September 1940 and 16 May 1941, which is hardly surprising. Indeed, with in excess of 18,000 tons of high explosive aimed at it, London had more than nine times rained down on it than the second-worst hit city in Britain, which was Liverpool. Birmingham, Glasgow,

Plymouth and Bristol, and their associated neighbourhoods, all endured more bombing than Coventry. But, significantly, damage was more widely spread. In just two major attacks, Coventry had 818 tons of high explosive hurled at it. The first of the attacks focused entirely on a compact area at the city's heart. Behind Coventry in the table, in descending order, stand Portsmouth, Southampton, Hull, Manchester, Belfast, Sheffield, Newcastle, Nottingham and Cardiff.

In Coventry as elsewhere, there were people who felt that they would never be able to forgive the Germans for all they had done. However, a healthy number reserved their enmity for the country's high command rather than the people who lived in its streets, especially after British bombing raids across Germany were stepped up.

Surprisingly, soon after the Blitz, a spirit of reconciliation began to emerge. At first, it was in a small way, like a flickering candle. The Coventry branch of the Peace Pledge Union objected when the *Daily Express* exhorted air chiefs to 'bomb back and bomb hard'. A letter published in the *New Statesman* outlined their point of view: 'The general feeling is that of horror and a desire that no other peoples shall suffer as they have done'.

Some like-minded people got together even before the war had ended to form a society called the German Circle. Their aim was to study the German language and culture to understand better the human face of those they called enemies.

Twenty years after the Blitz, when the Cold War between Soviet Russia and its satellite states and the western powers was at its most tense, Coventry Cathedral sent a working party to Dresden, which by then was tucked behind the Iron Curtain in East Germany. It was a reciprocal gesture after

German workers had visited Coventry some four years before. Before long, the cities with their shared suffering were twinned to help cement forgiveness and reconciliation.

As Coventry experienced the final days of the war, there was a sense of community that clearly would not be broken. When it finally came, VE Day was celebrated by thousands of people who congregated around the cathedral tower. Many took the opportunity to climb to its belfry and look out over the city to mourn the loss of its medieval glories and to wonder what would one day replace them. Once again, the events of 14 November 1940 were at the forefront of their minds. Mary Bloomfield, whose recollections have helped tell this story, and her husband Ted grieved once more for his best friend Ken who burned to death that night. In her diary, Mary wrote: 'Never again, I hope, will it be necessary to have a V-day. Surely another war will destroy civilisation.'

# Chapter Thirteen

# 'They sowed the wind and now they must reap the whirlwind'

*Sir Arthur 'Bomber' Harris*

In the outrage that rippled across Britain and the world after the Coventry Blitz there were numerous cries for vengeance. Naturally, those in Bomber Command – the attacking front line against Nazi Germany in the absence of a land war – were ready for vengeance. But as much as any pilot wanted to rain down bombs on Germany, British bombers were in fact incapable of pulling off such a feat with any impact. Despite claims to the contrary, British bombing was notoriously inaccurate.

Unlike their German counterparts, British aeroplanes lacked sophisticated equipment that could guide them to their destinations. Navigation still depended on dead reckoning – that is, mathematically calculating a position by using a previously determined 'fix', which was far from infallible, especially in the low-lying cloud that tended to dog northern Europe.

It was common practice in Germany, as it was in Britain, to light decoy fires in empty pasture to draw enemy aeroplanes and there were also simulated urban streets. (England had 792 static decoys in England at 593 locations during the Second World War.) As the conflict wore on, German anti-aircraft gunners sited in the vicinity of decoy fires stayed silent so that they did not reveal the true location of the target, although this was an unpopular ruse with residents who then felt like sitting ducks. It was, however, sufficient to mislead many British crews, who achieved few if any gains, and the missions they undertook were costly in terms of both men and machines.

Indeed, such were the limitations of the fliers in those early years of the war that the possibility of scaling back or even scrapping Bomber Command was at one stage seriously considered. It was some time before bombers could wreak havoc over Germany in the way the Luftwaffe had over Britain – although when the time came, their activities were every bit if not more shocking.

Following the raid on Coventry, there was something of a step change in the way raids against Germany were conducted. The bombing might have been labelled 'strategic' by those who undertook it, but initially the response seemed comparatively paltry, given the scale of the destruction in Coventry, and was troublingly inconsistent.

On the night of 15 November 1940, a combined force of sixty-seven Hampdens, Wellingtons and Whitleys were dispatched to Hamburg in two separate waves, leaving eight hours apart. Local records reveal that sixty-eight fires were started and that substantial damage was caused at the shipyard there. Twenty-six people were killed, more than 100 were injured and hundreds of homes were destroyed.

At the same time, a fifty-six-strong force comprising mostly Blenheim bombers peppered Luftwaffe airfields in occupied countries. Outstandingly, there were no RAF losses and the evening's work was considered something of a triumph. But the following night, it was a different story. This time, in poor weather, only sixty of 130 aircraft heading to Hamburg made it to the target zone, causing six fires, killing two people and damaging only a few score of houses. Other aircraft that had peeled off from the main force notched up some small-scale victories, but eight planes were lost.

It was hardly surprising, then, that something altogether more prestigious with better impact was called for as tangible retribution. A month after the Coventry Blitz, there was a raid on Mannheim, planned as a momentous turnaround for British fortunes in the aerial war. The largest force sent to any single target was assembled. Only bad weather prevented the number of bombers – 134 – from being increased.

But an attempt to raise fires across the city by the first wave of Wellington bombers failed and subsequent squadrons of aircraft dropped bombs sporadically, mostly in residential areas. Before the night was out, thirty-four people had died and the railway station, a school and two hospitals were damaged at the cost of seven British aeroplanes. All the while, Luftwaffe aeroplanes were causing devastation in a number of British cities in a way that Bomber Command seemed unable to replicate.

In February, the Air Ministry suggested a different strategy, that of bombing German oil refineries and synthetic oil plants to curb the Reich's military capabilities. With industrial production in Britain now moderate to good, more aeroplanes than ever before could be spared for the campaign.

For four months, bombers tried to annihilate significant industrial hubs, but there was little evidence that the plan was working. Then attentions were turned to U-boats, which were inflicting terrible losses on British shipping. Ports became prime targets, as the bombers targeted the submarines when they were in dock. For the bombers, which still lacked any measure of refined target-finding equipment, it was good news. Shorelines were generally easier to spot from an aircraft, so navigation and accuracy were at last enhanced. However, German planning was ahead of the Air Ministry. The change in tactics prompted the Germans to invest in swiftly built concrete pens for their submarines, to which boats and crews retired in heavy raids. Although the population of the targetted ports inevitably suffered, the U-boats were safe to fight another day. Bomber Command's plan to make the seas safer for the Royal Navy was shelved after it was shown that there was no discernible drop in U-boat production or operations.

The scope for the RAF at this point was broad. Clearly, it wanted to bomb Germany, but it also had targets in France, Italy, Norway and Holland in its sights. There were significant battleships to attack, mines to lay, dams to bomb and, inevitably, more leaflets to drop to drive the Allied message home to German and occupied populations. But for some time there was no discernible blueprint to follow.

In the middle of 1941, some clear ideas about bombing policy were formed at the Air Ministry. At its heart was the certainty that German morale was being severely dented by British bombing attacks and that this could be the key to defeating Hitler. Wrecking the transport system that was needed to carry German soldiers to and from the eastern front after the invasion of Russia in June 1941 was equally deemed to be a priority. Isolating the Ruhr where so much of the Reich's military equipment was manufactured was vital.

Henceforth, the targets on moonlit nights were railway installations, particularly those around the Ruhr. On dark nights, it was cities that were bombed – in particular, Hamburg, Bremen, Hanover, Frankfurt, Mannheim and Stuttgart. The raids were regular but relatively small scale.

In July 1941, the Chiefs of Staff declared their support for the role of Bomber Command and outlined why its role was crucial in any victory over Germany:

'We must first destroy the foundations upon which the German war machine runs – the economy which feeds it, the morale which sustains it, the supplies which nourish it and the hopes of victory which inspire it ... It is in bombing on a scale undreamt of in the last war that we find the new weapon on which we must principally depend for the destruction of German economic life and morale.'

However, German night fighters became increasingly better at picking a bomber out of the night sky. Bomber Command's size remained stagnant as additional aeroplanes and crew only just about kept pace with the heavy losses incurred. At the same time, the inaccuracy of Bomber Command was now being scrutinised at Whitehall.

The citizens of some German cities hit in early raids expressed genuine surprise that a force of tens or even hundreds of aeroplanes had been used against them. Most felt that just three or five aeroplanes were responsible for the limited damage left behind and believed that Allied claims of vast air fleets ranging against Germany were nothing more than 'Churchill's propaganda'.

Meanwhile, the government had received independent reports about the aftermath of raids from neutral countries. Claims of uncanny accuracy made by Bomber Command simply did not bear scrutiny. Much later, one group captain candidly admitted that to find a target in Germany at night was far beyond bomber crews at the time, no matter how brave and skilled they were. Even if crews could pin-point where they were on a map, the bombs would still fall awry to the tune of some five or seven miles. Three bombs in every hundred got within five miles of the target, he declared.

When the anomaly was noticed by Churchill's adviser Frederick Lindemann, a civil servant was given the task of looking at photographic evidence to assess just how close bombs were dropping to their designated targets. Photographic reconnaissance made after raids was in its infancy. The photographs used were taken by the bombers themselves as they unleashed their cargoes. Some 650 photographs were reviewed, garnered from 100 separate raids during July 1941. The results made for gloomy reading.

It was indeed true that only one bomb in three was dropped within five miles of the target – and that ratio plummeted if it was a moonless night. To make matters worse, a good number of aeroplanes that took off did not reach their targets. The statistics were only culled from aeroplanes that did. The unspoken question was, were the lives of the pilots and crews and the loss of the aeroplanes really worthwhile?

The one positive note in the report was the figures reflecting the bombing of French ports. There was a high success rate here, undoubtedly thanks to the ease to which the pilots could locate them. The author of the document was David Bensusan-Butt and it became known as the Butt report.

With this sword of Damocles hanging over him, Sir Richard Peirse – Commander-in-Chief of Bomber Command – began looking for better results and expanded the agenda that had been laid before him by the Air Ministry. Consequently, the first raid on Nuremberg took place in October 1941 involving some 152 aircraft. Some of the British crews conceded that they had bombed villages a few miles outside of Nuremberg.

Indeed, Nuremberg itself suffered only one fatality and six casualties, with limited damage.

However, in Lauingen, a village sixty-five miles away, the residents suffered a four-hour onslaught involving 200 high explosives and 700 incendiaries. Many other bombs fell in surrounding fields. Four people died, including the mayor who had a heart attack when he saw the village ablaze. Needless to say, there were no industrial targets in the vicinity. A total of thirteen British aeroplanes were lost that night.

Undaunted, Peirse assembled a mighty 169 aircraft to bomb Berlin on 7 November 1941, almost a year after the Coventry raid. The weather was poor and this might explain why just seventy-three aircraft found the target. When they did, the bombs were widely scattered and failed to unduly shake the capital. Some public buildings were affected, but not in such a way that would hinder the German war effort. Eleven people were killed, but, perhaps more significantly for the British, twenty-one aircraft were lost, an eighth of the number involved that night. It was the last major raid on Berlin until January 1943.

Winston Churchill called Peirse in to share with him overarching concerns about the efficacy of Bomber Command. The Prime Minister made it clear that, after he laid his views before the Cabinet, its very future was in the balance. For the time being, only limited operations would take place to conserve manpower and squadron sizes, as losses were once again in danger of outrunning new supplies.

It was, of course, a momentous winter. America entered the war in December after Pearl Harbor was attacked by the Japanese. In an extraordinary move, Hitler declared war on the United States, legitimising fighting by US forces in Europe on behalf of the Allies.

British colonies toppled like dominoes to the powerful Japanese forces seeking supremacy in the Pacific, while the fortunes of the Allies fighting in North Africa swung wildly between success and failure. The limited numbers of aeroplanes under British control were clearly going to be stretched more than ever before.

A change of face at the top of Bomber Command to meet these fresh challenges was perhaps not unexpected. Peirse was not sacked. His new job was in Southeast Asia, where a broad array of entirely different problems presented themselves.

In his place came Air Chief Marshal Sir Arthur Harris. Crucially, a week prior to his appointment the Air Ministry issued a directive that, in the absence of any success with targeted bombing, area bombing was now in order. Previously, civilian deaths and damage to workers' homes were seen as collateral. Now it was a tactic. The aim was to break the morale of the civil population, especially those who worked in industry. Interestingly, it was generally thought that destroying houses would undermine morale better than the deaths of friends and neighbours.

Perhaps with these orders in mind, when he took over as Commander-in-Chief in 1942, 'Bomber' Harris spoke in dark and biblical terms about the terror he had planned for the Germans. Hitler and his men had been under a 'childish delusion' that they could bomb at will and not be bombed back, he said. (He was possibly referring to a public pledge made by Luftwaffe chief Hermann Göring that no enemy plane would fly over Reich territory.) The RAF had already proved him wrong and Harris had big plans to do more of the same: 'At Rotterdam, London, Warsaw and half a hundred other places they put their rather naive theory into operation. They sowed the wind and now they must reap the whirlwind.'

Harris was keen to disprove those who maintained that bombing could never win a war. 'It has never been tried yet,' he insisted. 'We shall see.'

He quickly revealed that he believed it far easier to burn a city down than to blow it up and was considering inflating the number of incendiaries used to achieve this.

Technology along the same lines as that which had made the Coventry raid such a success for the Luftwaffe was now available to the Royal Air Force. A navigational aid known as Gee was being introduced to keep aeroplanes on course, although it struggled in the face of more distant targets because of the curvature of the earth. Aircraft in the first wave were fitted with Gee to ensure that the bombers reached the right locality.

One of the first victims of new thinking and enhanced capability at Bomber Command was Lubeck, which was attacked on 28 March by 234 aircraft, of which twelve were lost. A few days afterwards, Hitler's propaganda chief Josef Goebbels acknowledged in his dairy that the damage was 'really enormous' and the destruction 'horrible'.

'We can't get away from the fact that the English air-raids have increased in scope and importance; if they can be continued on these lines, they might conceivably have a demoralising effect on the population,' he wrote.

The RAF proceeded to drop leaflets on Germany referring to the Lubeck raid. The leaflets read: 'British bombers last night attacked a number of places on the German coast, above all the town of Lubeck – civilians suffered some injuries.

'The RAF dropped [many times more bombs] as the Luftwaffe used on Coventry a year ago. That is also eight times as many [bombs] as the Luftwaffe discharged over England in the whole month of March.'

Lubeck was not attacked again after an appeal by the Red Cross, which used the port facilities there. In response to the burning of Lubeck, the Luftwaffe mounted the Baedecker raids, attacks on historic British cities attracting more than three stars in a tourist guide, which included Exeter, Canterbury and York, among others.

'There is no other way of bringing the English to their senses,' Hitler told a reluctant Goebbels. 'They belong to a class of human beings to whom you can talk only after you have knocked out their teeth.'

Still, Harris stuck to his task, mindful of the need to redeem the reputation of Bomber Command. The first 1,000-bomber raid took place in May 1942, and was directed against Cologne. It was not easier to put that many aircraft together. The force comprised only 469 night bombers in total, as well as seventy-eight day bombers. All damaged aeroplanes had to be repaired. Without co-operation from the Royal Navy and its bombers which were devoted primarily to hunting U-boat, Harris was dependent on trainee pilots and training aeroplanes as well as their instructors, plus a contingent from Fighter Command to make up the numbers.

A new tactic of bomber streaming was also introduced in this attack. It meant every aeroplane followed a similar path, each having its own take-off time and prescribed height to prevent collisions – which had previously accounted for a great number of losses. The hope was that the sight of massed bombers would overawe German anti-aircraft gunners. The planes would then cause massive destruction, as well as providing triumphal headlines at home. The capacity of aeroplanes was improving, with some now carrying 4,000-lb bombs. By 1943, Lancasters, newly in service and still restricted in number, were able to carry explosives double that size.

The time taken for the raid was also cut to help minimise airborne casualties. The plan was that people of Cologne, huddled in deep shelters, would be bombed every other second for an hour and a half rather than all night long. As a result, there were 469 deaths, the largest number of people yet killed in a raid by Bomber Command, and 13,000 homes were destroyed.

Afterwards, the spires of Cologne's gorgeous Gothic cathedral remained upright and iconic, much as had been the case in Coventry. Likewise, the city's industry that had been damaged in the raid was back to work soon afterwards.

Before the night was over, forty-one aircraft had been lost; with sixteen shot down by flak above Cologne, two lost to a collision and the rest probably claimed by night fighters either over the city or on the journey to and from the mission. Churchill had said he would tolerate a 10 per cent loss – that is, 100 aeroplanes – so there must have been a sense of relief at the figures. But it was the loss of crews that had the most demoralising effect on those who survived, rather than the perceived success or failure of the mission.

There were two more 1,000-bomber raids in June: one on Essen at the start of the month and the second on Bremen, at its close. Essen was as usual shrouded in an industrial haze, which made the job of the bombers considerably harder. There was scattered rather than intensive bombing resulting in the loss of thirty-one aeroplanes. Results were better in Bremen, where a stiff breeze helped to fan the flames, but this time forty-eight aircraft were lost.

Lessons were learned during these raids. Gee had not solved all the problems that beset Bomber Command; some crews were better than others at finding targets, a skill that improved with experience. But many pilots and navigators did not stay alive long enough to perfect it.

\* \* \*

Although every man that was lost throughout the war caused much pain, a number of families suffered disproportionately as the ranks of fliers were reduced by crashes over enemy territory or on take-off or landing at home bases. The Garland family was among them.

In 1940, twenty-one-year-old Donald Garland was posthumously awarded the Victory Cross after bombing a canal bridge in Holland, hoping to thwart the German invasion.

Two years later, his brother Desmond, also a pilot, was presumed drowned at the age of twenty-seven, after his Manchester aircraft crashed into the sea off the French coast. Another brother, John, who was an instructor, died early in 1943, aged thirty-two and is buried in Suffolk. Patrick, the only one of the brothers who married, was thirty-six when he was killed after his Spitfire flipped over on landing in January 1945. His wife of ten years, Mollie, went to live with his widowed mother Winifred, or Mater as she was known, in London's Archway Road. Their father, also called Patrick, was a military surgeon who had died before the war.

Two of three brothers who died in the Second World War are buried in the same grave: Philip Herbert, who was aged twenty-six, and twenty-year-old Gerald lie together in Theale churchyard, Berkshire. They were both Flying Officers with the Royal Air Force Volunteer Reserve.

Philip was part of a photographic reconnaissance unit and was killed on 20 January 1942, while Gerald perished when his Halifax crashed on take-off on 14 February 1943. Their twenty-one-year-old brother Richard, who was also a pilot, was in 211 Squadron, which operated in the Middle East and took a pounding from the Luftwaffe when it was sent to defend Greece. He was the first of the trio to die, on 13 April 1941, and is buried in Phaleron, Greece.

Losses of this magnitude usually bring a sudden end to a family's story. For the Meikle family, there was a witness to carry theirs forward, who lived for decades after her brothers died. In this case, two out of the three were fliers.

When Flight Sergeant David Meikle perished as his stricken Stirling bomber crash-landed after limping back from a Second World War air raid, his mother Phyllis retired to her bedroom to grieve for two days in darkness and solitude. When she emerged, grey-faced but determined to make the best of things, no more than countless other mothers had endured up to the time of her son's death on 12 October 1943. But it was a grim ritual that she repeated twice more before peace broke out as Phyllis and her family, who lived in Hornchurch, in Essex, suffered fearful personal loss.

Paratrooper Lieutenant Ian Meikle, of the Royal Artillery, died on 21 September 1944 at Arnhem while Phyllis's youngest son Colin, a flight sergeant with the Royal Air Force Volunteer Reserve, was killed when his Hurricane crashed in India on 6 June 1945, after victory had been declared in Europe but before Japan was beaten. David and Colin were both twenty-one while Ian was twenty-four.

Phyllis courageously masked her devastation, not least for her youngest daughter Janice, who was still a child when the war finished. Much later Janice recalled her mother as noticeably happy, upbeat and 'an absolute dynamo'.

> My mother always said to me, never say 'Why did it happen to me?' Bad things happen to everyone. Never look back and don't be sorry for yourself.

She believed it was a just war. Things were very different then. A whole generation of people had been ruined in the First World War, when she had lost a brother.

My mother was a wonderful woman, very maternal. She wasn't shallow. She told me, 'You have got to enjoy life, don't worry about things you can't change.'

She had absolute faith but I found it completely unbelievable when she described how she would be going through a gate to heaven and the boys would be waiting for her.

It wasn't until I was in my sixties that I realised she probably didn't believe that herself. She made sure I suffered as little as possible.

Every five years, on the anniversary of Armistice Day, Janice's mother put a notice in *The Times* and the *Daily Telegraph*, listing the boys' names and words taken from the Bible: 'In their lives they were lovely and pleasant, And in death they were not divided'.

Largely, the family's coping strategies worked well and Janice's childhood was only occasionally marred by the weight of grief. Her parents wept together on holiday in the Isle of Wight in the wake of wild celebrations following VJ Day in 1945. Janice also saw her Scottish-born father Ormiston, a successful heating engineer, cry when he visited Ian's grave in Holland soon after the war. Years later, disabled by old age and senility, Ormiston lived with Janice. One night, he leaped out of bed, rushed into her son's room and said: 'Come on, Ian, I will get you out before the Germans get you.' After Ormiston's death, Janice, who now lives in Wivenhoe, Essex, received letters from ex-servicemen who were given financial assistance by him following the war.

Phyllis was already forty-eight when Janice was born. As well as the three boys, there was an older sister, April, who became nun and then a teacher. When she found out she was pregnant against medical advice, Phyllis took her four teenage children walking in Snowdonia and told them: 'It isn't what any of us wanted but we must all pretend we do and then it will be alright.'

For Janice, the scars of the war deaths still remain. 'I felt I had a ghost family that I didn't really belong to, although I always enjoyed hearing stories about what they got up to pre-war from my mother and playing with their toys.' She learned that the boys were sporty, clever and lived life to the full. Their home was a rambling Victorian house with a tennis court and a pool and they all enjoyed a comfortable, middle-class existence.

With Hornchurch close to London and an air base, Janice, then aged five, was evacuated at the outbreak of war to Wales where she suffered regular beatings. Her mother saw the bruises when she hitchhiked from London for a surprise visit and took Janice away immediately, dispatching her to boarding school.

'I have very clear memories of my middle brother David because he was the one who used to play with me,' Janice recalled and, with hindsight, she believes he was concerned both about the consequences of bombing city populations and his chances of survival. She can also recall the tinned peaches and nylons that her youngest brother Colin brought back from the United States where he learned to fly. From the Dutch family who housed him in the early days of Operation Market Garden, she learned that Ian was gallant and kind.

For her part, she always tempered her behaviour because of the family's loss: 'I always felt I had to be jolly nice and not complain about boarding school, which I absolutely hated. My mother would have been horrified if she thought I thought like that.'

While at boarding school, Janice was told about each death by her mother, although she cannot recall her response. Janice was then haunted by nightmares in which her brothers returned, as she had fervently hoped they would, but were ravaged by terrible injuries.

Shut away from the war in a convent, April suffered depression. She later left and undertook a successful academic career.

In childhood, Phyllis had known grinding poverty, going to school with barefooted children and later teaching gym to women workers at the Bryant & May match factory in the East End. After the war, she became a liaison officer between foster parents and the council – and once teenager Janice questioned her about wearing tailor-made clothes, a hat and gloves to visit poor women with few possessions.

'It would be offensive to dress down,' said Phyllis. 'Besides, they all know what happened to me, dear.'

Every year, they would decorate the tree on Christmas Eve and shed a few tears as they talked about the boys. On Christmas Day, Phyllis would host a joyful party that filled the house with friends. 'I asked my mother once, "Did Colin have to go? He was only nineteen,"' said Janice. 'He enjoyed it so much and he wanted to go,' replied her mother.

Janice can only recall one occasion in her childhood when Phyllis appeared bitter and it occurred after the death of a garden bird. As Janice wept uncontrollably, her mother snapped: 'You didn't cry like this when your brothers died.'

The emotional toll of the loss of her siblings still surprises Janice: 'I didn't think about it for years but it affects me more as I get older.' Recently, she found photographs of her youngest brother Colin, who closely resembled her grandson, as he started university, and there was an overwhelming sadness is for what might have been.

David is buried in Cambridge, Ian in Arnhem and Colin, whose fate was for months shrouded in mystery, at the Delhi War Cemetery. The Meikles visited all the graves at least once, although, said Janice, 'My mother didn't really hold with graves. She wasn't a person who held on to sorrow.'

To his men, the Commander-in-Chief was known as 'Butcher' Harris, not for his controversial bombing raids in which civilians were killed, but for his apparently hardhearted approach to the deaths of his men.

In fact, he held them in such esteem that he refused a knighthood when they were not given a medal of honour at the end of the war. By the end of the conflict, 55,573 men out of a total of 125,000 aircrew had been killed, a 44.4 per cent death rate. Statistically, one in six survived their first tour and one in forty their second. They were not expected to undertake a third. In addition to that, there were shocking injuries and a substantial number who became prisoners of war.

For Harris, the deaths were a daily reality. He took advice from mathematicians about how successful the raids might be to help weigh the odds, which might have meant altering routes, the height of flying or formations. But his faith in the old adage 'the bomber will always get through' was unshakeable.

A number of improvements increased the chances of survival for crews from 1942: a blind bombing device called

Oboe helped guide aeroplanes to their destinations with better accuracy than ever before; the H2S radar set finally replaced dead reckoning, giving pilots a better chance of finding their targets and getting home; and Pathfinders (aeroplanes which dropped an incendiary route for others to follow) were being used, despite an initial resistance from Harris, just as the German used them against Coventry. With the best equipment in the most durable aeroplanes, they would light up the target with 'concentrated incendiarism' as it was dubbed by Harris, so other aircraft could follow more easily in their wake.

Tinsel was used to flood the frequencies used by German night fighters, to distract pilots. Electronic equipment known as Mandrel was built to jam German radar. And, for a while, Window – strips of aluminium foil that created a cloud of false radar echoes later known as chaff – was scattered by incoming British aeroplanes successfully to mask their route, although the Germans quickly rumbled it.

Clunky, aged aircraft like the Manchester, Blenheim and Hampden bombers were replaced with new Lancasters and fast-moving Mosquitoes. The sturdy Wellington was relegated to other duties.

The survival statistics for crews finally looked better when the United States Air Force began pounding Germany, primarily during daylight hours. Both air forces had the fundamental aims behind their missions outlined at the Casablanca conference in January 1943 attended by all the Allied leaders: 'Your primary object will be the progressive destruction and dislocation of the German military, industrial, and economic system and the undermining of the morale of the German people to a point where their capacity for armed resistance is fatally weakened.'

But the Americans were not entirely in accord with Bomber Command about its avowed aim to destroy German cities. As early as 1942, Major Alexander Seversky, of the US Army Air Force, reflected on the flaws of the plan in his book *Victory Through Air Power.*

Although his message primarily outlined the risk the United States was exposed to by air power, he said the assumption that aerial bombardment would shatter popular morale was unfounded, the surprise result of this vital lesson they had now learned.

These facts are significant beyond their psychological interest. They mean that haphazard destruction of cities – sheer blows at morale – are costly and wasteful in relation to the tactical results achieved ...

Unplanned vandalism from the air must give way, more and more, to planned, predetermined destruction. More than ever the principal objectives will be critical aggregates of electric power, aviation industries, dock facilities, essential public utilities and the like.

This thinking prevailed as long as the US had confidence in its fleet of B17 'Flying Fortresses' armed with Norden bombsights that they felt could make precision bombing a reality. In fact, two raids against Schweinfurt, where crucial ball bearings necessary to make vehicles work were made, forced a change of heart. The raids were a failure and scores of bombers fell victim to German fighters. Afterwards, the USAAF joined Bomber Command in its general attacks against cities.

Other factors changed, too. After Germany was defeated at Stalingrad in February 1943, troops were transferred back to major cities, which were better defended with anti-aircraft guns than ever before.

And Bomber Command had another target to add to its array: the site where the V1 rockets were being developed. Even with modern navigational and bombing aids, Peenemünde, on the Baltic Coast, was an extremely small target.

Although there were many demands on his force, Harris remained set on the notion of bombing Berlin during the winter of 1943. At his disposal were aircraft in numbers he could once only have dreamed about, which carried outlandishly large tonnages of bombs. Despite the adverse weather conditions that they would bring, Harris needed the longer autumn nights of 1943 to bomb Berlin successfully.

Believing the policy would bring an early end to the war, Harris felt the destruction of two-and-a-half cities every month was both desirable and achievable. Yet, as Colonel Seversky predicted, repeated attacks did not bring the German capital to its knees in the way Harris had envisaged.

Regardless of the barrage let loose in night raids carried out by British bombers and daylight raids carried out by the Americans, life continued in Berlin, albeit with a sense of numbness. Offices still functioned and factories continued to produce armaments as best they could. The sense of shock that inevitably followed a big bombing raid anywhere ebbed away, even when the attacks continued. There was no collapse in morale, just as there had not been in London or Coventry. Rather, it was morale in Bomber Command that dipped as losses continued to accrue.

Although people were not moved to revolution by their experiences under the welter of British bombs, that is not to say that people were not terrified. One nurse in Cologne later recalled how many people caught fire and were running around 'like human torches'. In Hamburg, where a series of raids in the summer of 1943 spearheaded by the aptly named Operation Gomorrah killed as many as 50,000 people, one witness said:

> The scenes of terror in the firestorm area are indescribable. Children were torn away from their parents' hands by the force of the hurricane and whirled into the fire. People who thought that they had escaped fell down, overcome by the devouring heat, and died in an instant. Refugees had to make their way over the dead and dying. The sick and the infirm had to be left behind by the rescuers as they themselves were in danger of burning.

In Berlin, the effects of the bombs were equally shocking. One diarist at the time noted: '[W]e came upon places through which it was impossible to pass by car. Craters filled with water, heaps of rubble, firehoses, ... and convoys of lorries blocked the streets, where thousands of those rendered homeless were searching the ruins, trying to rescue some of their possessions, or were squatting on the pavements and being fed from field kitchens.'

Although there was something of a respite for German cities in the spring of 1944, as plans were being laid for the invasion in June, worse was yet to come. The bombing of Dresden on 13 February became a benchmark much as Coventry had done. The primary aim of Operation Thunderclap, as it was dubbed, was to bring the war to an early end by smashing remnants of the German war machine.

Dresden was an undoubtedly important communications point. Equally, the city was packed with refugees from the

Russian offensive in the east. A planned American daylight raid was called off because of bad weather, but that night 796 Lancasters and nine Mosquitoes dropped 1,478 tons or high explosive and 1,182 tons of incendiaries in two separate waves. The ensuing firestorm killed at least 40,000 people, and the total was probably closer to 50,000.

One woman recalled the horror:

> The firestorm is incredible, there are calls for help and screams from somewhere but all around is one single inferno. To my left I suddenly see a woman. I can see her to this day and shall never forget it. She carries a bundle in her arms, it is her baby. She runs, she falls, and the child flies in an arc into the fire … Insane fear grips me and from then on I repeat one simple sentence to myself, 'I don't want to burn to death'.

By now, Churchill appeared to be having doubts about this no-holds-barred tactic of carpet bombing. The act has since been labelled a war crime, as the military purpose of the raid was closely questioned. Indeed, Winston Churchill, thought by many to have been the greatest Briton ever to have lived, has been accused of being a war criminal.

Detailed consideration of what occurred at Dresden and elsewhere did not occur for decades after the war, with attention deflected by the horror of the Holocaust. The psychological harm wrought by Fascism and its associated crimes dulled the voices of generations. Certainly, the bombing of Germany in the latter years of the war following improvements in technology had shocking results. Around 600,000 German civilians died, including 76,000 German children.

For his part, 'Bomber' Harris did not acknowledge any barbarism in the actions taken by Bomber Command over Germany in general, or in Dresden in particular. The policy to bomb German cities was already instituted before he became Commander-in-Chief, he insisted. It was nothing personal, he said, he was merely carrying out orders: 'I lived in a shower of directives from the day I started to the last day of the war. The directive when I took over was the one that I wasn't specifically to aim at anything unless ordered to do so except to blast German cities as a whole.'

If he became unpopular in some quarters for his blinkered devotion to area bombing, he was backed wholeheartedly by his men. Characteristically, he sent robust and vivid messages to buoy up pilots and crews before they embarked on another dangerous mission over Germany. 'Let him have it right on the chin,' was one of the mildest. 'Tonight you are to go to the big city. You have the opportunity to light a fire in the belly of the enemy and burn his black heart out,' was another, dispatched shortly before one of the Berlin raids.

He and others would say the bombing of German towns and cities was as a direct result of what happened in Coventry and other British cities that had been Blitzed. Certainly, survivors from the attack in Coventry would have recognised much of the trauma that German people endured in the final years of the war; injuries, shock, the loss of loved ones, the fear of another raid, lack of food, shelter and warmth and an uncertain future.

# Conclusion

The raid on Coventry was a triumph for the Luftwaffe. A British city was comprehensively crushed in the biggest raid ever mounted and the German bomber force returned to home bases virtually unscathed. Airmen were told that it was the first of a series of crushing blows that would be delivered to Britain, as reprisals for small-scale bombing on German cities. But, for reasons unknown, the Luftwaffe failed to capitalise on the strike against Coventry. Seeking other fruitful targets, it didn't immediately return to take advantage of its aerial superiority, and the Luftwaffe failed to appreciate that time was not on its side.

Before the raid on Coventry, Luftwaffe pilots had greater fears about take-offs and landings at weather-affected airstrips than they ever did about meeting an RAF fighter in the darkened skies over Britain.

Soon the momentum changed, thanks to the leaps in technology accomplished in Britain. From January 1941, the accuracy of anti-aircraft guns was dramatically improved, after data about incoming fliers detected by radar was passed back to the gun operations room. Now, British air chiefs had a far better idea of how many aeroplanes were coming and where they were headed. The secrets inadvertently spilled

248

after German codes were broken at Bletchley Park also gave British aeroplanes a clear advantage. No one in Germany appreciated how efficient the early warning radar system developed by Britain would be.

Following the creation of *Knickebein* and *X-Gerät* – both masterful technologies for the era – there was a fatal complacency in the Luftwaffe about the infallibility of the systems. Very soon, the beams used by the Germans to steer them to Coventry were compromised by British jammers. Afterwards, when the beam was detected, British fliers in newly improved aeroplanes would follow it to meet the enemy head on.

German authorities also committed the same error that the British did later on, in assuming that the effects of a substantial bombing raid were fulsome and final, as far as industrial output was concerned. In fact, Coventry factories got back to work quickly, even those that had sustained damage. Had German bombers returned the night after the November Blitz to 'finish the job', it might have been a different story.

If the city's manufacturers had been put out of commission, then North Africa would have been lost for want of equipment, Russia might have been defeated and the D-Day landings might never have happened.

If Coventry had been annihilated in 1940, then 1,066 rapid Mosquito fighter bombers would not have been tested at RAF Ansty, just outside the city. Nor would Armstrong Siddeley have been able to experiment with the first jet engines there in 1942. But as it was, the lull in serious air raids gave everyone the time to repair themselves and their surroundings as best they could.

Much of the blame for the cumulative failings of the Luftwaffe can be laid at the door of its commander Hermann Göring.

Deficient in tactics and strategy and impervious to criticism, Göring focused solely on attack, which led to a disproportionate weakness in the fighter arm of his organisation. Ultimately, there were not enough German fighters on hand to tackle the British and, later, American bombers.

This blind faith in the efficacy of bombers also bred discord between fighter and bomber wings, with the heavy attack aeroplanes laid bare by the commitment of too few escort aircraft. According to one report produced for the British government in 1948, anyone who was alert to the threat from exceptional British fighters was slapped down.

> Göring himself was dazzled by his own self esteem and he and the whole of the Luftwaffe were subconsciously affected in their judgement by the outpouring of the German propaganda department.
>
> The German fighter men had begun to see the possibility of a tough adversary in the Spitfire and Hurricane but the series of easy victories from Poland onwards had prejudiced their judgement in assessing the capabilities of the Royal Air Force. Indeed, anybody who as much as hinted at the possibility of a fighter superior to the Me 109 incurred the risk of the serious disapproval of his superiors.

The raid on Coventry led to a series of unforeseen consequences. It was used to fashion American public opinion in favour of Britain and against Germany, for example, at a time when many in the United States were resisting the growing clamour to join the Allies. After the raid, the *New York Times* had no doubt that President Roosevelt should commit more fully to Britain in her hour of need.

The disaster of Coventry is a clear warning to America to rush the material aid we have pledged to give and which our people overwhelming desire to give.

There is no time for us to send at our leisure. The British are now more than ever dependent on America to increase their airplane strength which can, in time, defeat the Hitler challenge to our world.

The inevitable loss of aircraft production in Coventry will have to be made good by American factories: losses of British ships will have to be replaced by American shipyards; shortages of British equipment will have to be repaired from American stores.

If the destruction of Coventry awakens our people to a new sense of Britain's danger the victims of this horror will not have died in vain.

American armaments did indeed continue to pour into Britain following the Coventry raid, but the United States did not join hostilities until after the attack on Pearl Harbor by the Japanese in December 1941. And the attack against Coventry helped to justify a series of destructive raids against Germany carried out until the collapse of the Third Reich, with extraordinary human cost. One raid against Hamburg in 1943 killed 100 times more people than in Coventry.

But the blindness created in the minds of leaders in Britain after disasters like that of Coventry might also have harmed the Allied cause. With the idea of 'collective punishment' on its mind, formed partially as a result of the Coventry raid, Bomber Command failed to focus on the destruction of Germany's oil industry which might feasibly have brought an early end to the war. The same theory exists regarding US bombing; that had the ball bearing factory at

Schweinfurt been successfully flattened, the cogs in the German war machine might have ground to a halt. Both are highly speculative premises.

In Coventry, itself there were changes afoot. As early as March 1941, there was a decision to rebuild the wrecked cathedral although it was more than a decade later that 200 architects displayed their designs at King Henry VIII School, itself rebuilt after the Easter Blitz. Building work began in 1954 on the chosen design by Sir Basil Spence and was completed in 1962. The cathedral finally opened seven years and eighty-one days after the start of its first excavation.

On 25 May 1962, the *Church Times* celebrated the opening of the new cathedral by saying that Coventry would become 'a city of pilgrimage, pageantry and colour' for its guests, who included royalty, and the Archbishop of Canterbury read the first sermon.

Response to the new building varied from the effusive to the affronted. The *Daily Herald* observed that 'It is a work of art entirely in touch with the times in which it has been created'. The design was welcomed as timely by the *Daily Mail*, too, which said, 'Significantly it looms over its bombed out medieval predecessor, a sign perhaps that the church really has stepped into the space age'. However, the *Daily Telegraph* branded it 'a terrible disappointment', while the *Daily Express* correctly predicted that 'it [would] send some people up the wall.'

The city got a new pedestrianised shopping centre – one of the first in Europe – a museum, houses and ultimately a university. Fittingly, a Phoenix, the mythical creature that rises from its own ashes, is the subject of one of its civic sculptures.

Coventry remained a 'motor city' until the Seventies, after which most manufacturers deserted it, leaving behind a workforce perceived to have a poor history in industrial relations. The Labour politican Anthony Crosland was once moved to observe that 'the most militant local parties are not in the old industrial areas, but either in the newer high-wage engineering areas or in middle-class towns; Coventry or Margate are the characteristic strongholds'. With the insulation against economic hardship provided by the car companies gone, Coventry people worked hard to bring the city back to prosperity by the Nineties.

Although the concrete, boxy architecture that dominates Coventry is a constant reminder of the Blitz, more unexpected mementoes still come to light occasionally. Unexploded bombs were found around the city in 1978, 2008 and 2009, but there were some more subtle consequences of that November night that are all too easy to miss.

On 11 May 1941, the entertainer George Formby, a cheeky comedian and ukele player, came to Coventry to perform for its bomb-battered population. In the audience was seven-year-old Alan Randall from Bedworth, who was so inspired by what he saw on stage that he went on to make his name as a George Formby impressionist. The likeness between the two men could not mask Alan's musical talent and he was hailed as a performer around the world before his death in Nuneaton in 2005.

More curiously still, the *Dr Who* theme tune has its roots in the bombing raids on Coventry. Its creator, Delia Derbyshire, was just three years old when she was caught up in the Blitz. Much later, she became a pioneer of electronic music and composed, among others, the characteristic sound of the theme tune to the long-running TV series. In an interview, she credited the sounds of warfare on the home front as an inspiration: 'I was there in the Blitz and it's come to me, relatively recently, that my love for abstract sounds [came from] the air-raid sirens: that's a sound you hear and you don't know the source of as a young child ... then the sound of the "all clear" – that was electronic music.'

After the Blitz, Delia moved to Preston where her parents once lived and the percussive sound of clogs on cobbles created when mill employees were going to work at dawn was another influence.

The story of Coventry's war is full of people like Delia, her parents and everyone whose life spiralled out of control after the three major bombing raids, especially the battering delivered in November. They became front-line soldiers without the means to defend themselves or their loved ones.

Although he had no special love of the city or its people – visiting Coventry no more than twice despite its importance – Winston Churchill remained aware of the cost exacted from them and other ordinary people in the battle to stop the spread of fascism. It was those in Coventry among others that he had in mind when he fashioned the following tribute.

'This is no war of chieftains or of princes, of dynasties or national ambition,' he said. 'It is a war of peoples and of causes. There are vast numbers, not only in this Island but in every land, who will render faithful service in this war, but whose names will never be known, whose deeds will never be recorded. This is a War of the Unknown Warriors.'

# Epilogue

Everyone who survived the Second World War had a different story to tell. For those who shared their memories of one terrible night and its consequences for this book, that tale began with an extraordinary episode, but it continued to evolve alongside the conflict. The sounding of the all-clear did not put them out of harm's way for the rest of the war.

Alan Hartley's brother Leslie – plucked from the sands at Dunkirk back in 1940 – died in North Africa in 1942 as he tried to dismantle a mine buried in the sand. His family were tortured with the knowledge he had a 'Dear John' letter in his pocket when he died from a girl breaking off their engagement. Had it been enough to disturb his concentration that day?

In 1943, Alan joined Transport Command and was based at Down Ampney in Hampshire where he serviced and supplied British aeroplanes after D-Day. With the reversal at Arnhem, when German soldiers got the better of British paratroopers, he lost good friends after crews he looked after were shot down. In peacetime, he was a keen footballer and later, a referee. He also campaigned for official recognition of the work done by nurses who flew from Down Ampney after D-Day to bring back wounded servicemen.

Known as 'Flying Nightingales', the women nursed casualties from the Battle of Normandy as they were ferried home.

Betty Daniel left school in 1944 at the age of thirteen. Although she wanted to be a hairdresser, she was dispatched to secretarial college to learn shorthand and typing. She worked for some months as a secretary, but quickly left for a job in a hardware shop, which she loved. Betty spent her early teenage years congregating with others outside the Saturday night dance at Dunlop's works club, which began at 7.00 p.m. and ended by 10.00 p.m.. To the mystification of Coventry people like herself, black American troops came out on the town one night, and their white counterparts the next. It was these soldiers who taught local girls in pleated skirts to jitterbug and jive. Betty and her friends, who were used to more sedate ballroom dancing, looked on in amazement.

(As well as Americans in Coventry – who disappeared before the D-Day landings in 1944 – there were German POWs in the area, who were detained at Arbury Hall in Nuneaton until 1948, and provided a source a labour during clearing and reconstruction work.)

Betty also went to her local youth centre, where she loved sports including netball and running and dancing. When she was fifteen, she met a man called John there, and they married in 1950. They had a son Robert, twins Nigel and John, another son Mark and triplets Anne, Jane and Mandy. Betty worked at Parkgate Primary School for fifty years, retiring in 2013, and was a long-standing volunteer Scout leader and swimming teacher in Coventry.

Mary Latham left Brico in 1942 to work at Alfred Herbert's in Exhall. But being desk-bound did not suit her and she missed the friendly banter she had previously had with colleagues. Eventually, she found a job at Massey Ferguson.

After devoting days to salvage work at BTH and nights to the St John Ambulance Brigade, John Sargent decided to make a more distinctive contribution to the war effort. He wanted to be a pilot, so he went to the RAF College Flying Training School at RAF Cranwell in Lincolnshire. He underwent tests for ten days, before going in front of an interview board. One of the interview board members was a director of Modern Machine Tools in Coventry who recognised John, a skilled machine toolmaker and, as such, a valuable worker. The next day, he was presented with a rail ticket back to Coventry, where he worked on apprentice wages despite his seniority until the end of the war.

After the war, John worked in a shop and then as a first aider at Keresley Colliery. Twice widowed, John was a keen gardener who devoted much of his retirement to the organic gardens at Ryton on Dunsmore.

Eileen Bees's brother William – who had pulled her from the path of flying glass during the November Blitz – died on 5 September 1944 when his tank was destroyed by Germans as he fought his way through Italy after the fall of Mussolini. Desperate to join the Navy as a submariner, William was turned down because of a perforated ear drum, and so he joined the Royal Armoured Corps instead. Later, the family learned that he had volunteered to join the fateful reconnaissance mission when someone else dropped out through illness.

Eileen and her family first knew about his death from a letter received from King George VI, which lay on the mantelpiece at their new home in Cleveland Road, Stoke until their father Thomas returned from work. 'We pray that your country's gratitude for a life so nobly given in its service may bring you some measure of consolation,' the letter said. In fact, the words proved scant consolation.

After the war, her mother Viola – after so much experience of giving birth herself – helped to deliver babies in the neighbourhood, including the record producer Pete Waterman. In 1953, Eileen married Coventry man Ken Bees who had been evacuated to his grandparents in Wales, where he witnessed the death of his grandmother after she fell and hit her head while putting up blackout material. Six weeks later, his grandfather died of natural causes. He was moved to strangers, where he was so less favoured than the children of the household that items sent by his mother were given to them rather than to him. When he told his mother he was going to run away, he was brought back to Coventry.

The loss of her father in the April Blitz, followed by the death of her grandfather, the following year, brought a radical change in circumstances for Marjorie Edge. Although Marjorie's mother Annie had a war widow's pension, she was still short of money, having lost her husband, who was the household's wage earner, and her father who had been a good gardener, in short order.

Annie moved the family to live behind an empty shop premises on Foleshill railway bridge where there was no garden, an outside lavatory, perpetual pollution from the steam trains and excessive noise from engines, banging doors and loud chatter. Annie got a job in the Lyon's café in Broadgate, a prefabricated building that remained in place for a number of years. By now, only Marjorie and her younger sister Eileen were living at home. Majorie's eldest sister, Vera, had married while her brother Raymond went into the Army and was sent to Egypt. Before she herself married, in 1950, Marjorie was a St John Ambulance Cadet and a Sea Ranger.

Christina and Len Stephenson returned to Coventry and marked VE Day with the conception of their only son, Gary.

Len and Cecilia Dacombe also returned to Coventry to bring up a family and ended up living in retirement at Leamington.

# The Coventry Blitz in Numbers

**Coventry at War Before, During and After the Blitz**

- 260,000 people lived in Coventry at the start of the war.
- 55 hours was the typical working week.
- 1 in every 7 bombers produced during the war came from a factory operated by the Rootes Group, based in Coventry.
- 1,029 Fairey bombers were built in British shadow factories in the war years, along with 300 Hawker Hurricanes, 330 Avro Lancaster bombers, 365 Airspeed Horsa gliders, 1,780 Handley Page Halifax bombers.
- 1,317 tank transporters were built by the British motor industry during the war years, along with 333,274 lorries, 14,543 ambulances, 421,039 motorcycles and 156,036 15-cwt trucks.
- 64 barrage balloons helped to defend Coventry on the night of the Blitz.
- 6,698 volunteers helped to defend Coventry during the Second World War, more than a third of whom were in the Air Raid Protection service.
- 65 per cent of people didn't carry gas masks according to a poll in October 1940, due to the complacency during the phoney war.

- 80,920 Anderson shelters were delivered to Coventry before the November raid.
- 170,344 places were available in shelters prior to the Blitz.

**The Damage**
- 377 air raid casualties were taken from bombed buildings by Coventry's St John Ambulance Brigade while records were being kept that night. More were treated and transported after records stopped being made.
- 300 gas mains, which were 4–24 inches in diameter, were damaged.
- 1,000 branch sewers were fractured.
- 350 roads were affected.
- An estimated 130 high explosives, five land mines, nine oil bombs, 17 delayed action bombs and about 2,500 incendiaries were dropped on the Daimler works in Radford, causing the biggest factory fire recorded in Britain at the time.
- £1,831 7 s 4d was the cost of the repairs at the Courtaulds factory in Foleshill Road after the Blitz, when damage was caused by two explosive bombs in particular and a number of incendiaries.

**The Emergency Services**
- 26 firemen working for Coventry Fire Brigade, the city's auxiliary fire brigade, the works brigades and those who travelled there from surrounding areas died during the November Blitz.
- 2 brigade tenders, 9 towing vehicles and 7 Home Office pumps were destroyed.

- 10 sergeants and 88 constables from Birmingham went to Coventry immediately after the Blitz to help keep law and order.
- 1 Inspector, 7 sergeants and 92 constables were sent from Worcestershire and Shropshire on 15 November for the same purpose.
- 43 St John Ambulance Brigade personnel were on duty on the night of the Blitz.

**Aid**
- 64 rescue parties were sent to Coventry following the Blitz.
- 40 ambulances were sent from other districts.
- 120 lorries were supplied by the regional traffic commissioner for carrying water, but 75 were sent back because there were not sufficient water tanks for them to use.
- 20,000 blankets were sent by special train from London.
- 11 feeding stations for Coventry evacuees opened in Northamptonshire.

# Bibliography and Further Information

**Books**

Churchill, Winston, *The Second World War* (New Ed.), Pimlico, London, 2002.

Harrisson, Tom, *Living Through the Blitz*, HarperCollins, London, 1975.

Jenkins, Roy, *Churchill*, Pan, London, 2002.

Jones, R. V., *Most Secret War*, Hamish Hamilton, London, 1978.

Lewis, Tim, *Moonlight Sonata*, Time Lewis & Coventry City Council, Coventry, 1990.

Longmate, Norman, *Air Raid*, Arrow Books, London, 1978.

Middlebrook, Martin & Everitt, Chris, *The Bomber Command War Diaries* (reprint), Midland Publishing, Hinckley, 2011.

Wakefield, *Kenneth, The First Pathfinders* (New Ed.), Crecy Publishing, Manchester, 1992.


**Newspaper and Magazine Archives**

*The Church Times*
*The Coventry Evening Telegraph*
*The Daily Mirror*
*The Daily Express*
*The Daily Worker*


**Other Resources**

The Coventry Blitz Resource Centre

SiteSafe Unexploded Ordnance (UXO) Desk Study by Zeltica for
Coventry City Council

**Websites**

www.historiccoventry.co.uk

# Index